The Modern Stoic Father

Ancient Virtues for Raising Resilient Kids in Today's Families

William T. Harrison

Table of Contents

Introduction

Fatherhood is a different experience for every dad. Although there are common denominators, when it comes to raising a child, each of us is on a different planet. However, there is one thing we all have in common: Parenthood is the most beautiful and challenging experience we will ever have. What kind of dad do we want to be? What parenting style do our children need? Throughout this book, we will search for the answers to these questions.

My name is William T. Harrison and, like you, I have been a navigator of the tumultuous seas they call parenting. Throughout even the stormiest moments, over many years, the ability to adapt is a fundamental tool for raising healthy children. And there, beneath the darkest clouds, Stoicism found me. This book is not only intended to be a guide, but, rather, a warm hug for parents who, like me, have felt the call of Stoicism and wish to integrate it with the complexities of modern parenting.

I remember those early days of parenting, when nights turned into days and diapers were changed, trying to stay calm in the midst of chaos. I found comfort in Stoic teachings after experiencing a personal tragedy in my 30s. The loss of a friend and the collapse of my joint venture threw me into a search for direction.

In ancient Greece, Zeno of Citium, the visionary behind Stoicism, lost his ship and merchandise during a storm, later finding himself in Athens with few resources. In his search for solace and wisdom, he immersed himself in the teachings of Socrates and the Cynics before finding his intellectual home in Stoicism.

Thanks to philosophy, Zeno discovered a complete approach to life, a set of ideas that embraced ethics, logic, and physics. Fascinated by Stoicism's ability to provide sound principles in the midst of adversity, he adopted this philosophy as a guide for his own life and founded the Stoic school in Athens. Zeno presented Stoicism as a lifeline, a philosophy that not only calms emotional storms, but also offers solid principles that allow human beings to lead a virtuous life.

Imagine Zeno, facing the waves of the sea and the storms of life, seeking philosophical answers in the dialogues of Socrates. These personal experiences influence him to create a philosophy that has stood the test of centuries.

Just as Zeno sought wisdom to overcome his challenges, we can apply Stoic principles to our own odyssey as parents. We will see throughout the book that Stoic ethics can guide our daily decisions as parents. Through constant decision-making, we carry out our existence. The vast majority of them are minor decisions, but, sometimes, life takes us by surprise and requires us to take transformative actions.

What benefits might we gain from discerning what we can and cannot control in the journey of parenthood? How much can having a modern stoic father add to our children's childhood? Is Stoic philosophy even applicable to parenting? Through these questions, I invite you to reflect on the connection between Stoic philosophy and parenting. Could it be that, like Zeno, we will find in Stoicism a beacon of wisdom to navigate the complexity of parenting in the modern world?

This book is for you, stoic father. Here you will find more than theory; you will find empathetic stories and practical advice that will guide you through every step of parenthood. I understand, share, and go through every dad's challenges daily. From the fear of not being good enough to the complications of conversations about growth and responsibility, each stage presents us with its own storm of uncertainties. The four Stoic virtues—wisdom, courage, justice, and temperance—become reliable beacons, lights that illuminate even the darkest corners of our insecurities.

In this literary journey, the central purpose is to immerse ourselves in the fundamental principles of Stoicism, highlighting the immense value and transformative capacity that the four virtues can bring to our lives. Thinking of a virtuous life as a motivation that invites us to explore the practical application of this ancient philosophy in daily decision-making, cultivating wisdom, courage, justice, and temperance in the very fabric of our existence as parents.

From small decisions to monumental challenges, we seek to illustrate how Stoicism can be a trusted guide in the odyssey of modern parenting. Recognizing the universal aspects of the parenting experience, we strive to transcend individual and cultural differences. And it will be in the differences where each one of us will find their way.

Looking at everyday life, we will see how to integrate Stoic concepts into real situations. I try to be not only a theoretical compendium, but also an empathetic and experienced companion on the journey of parenthood. The odyssey begins here. So, as you delve into these pages, think of me as a companion on your journey, ready to offer comfort when you need it and guidance when you seek answers.

I am excited to set sail with you toward parenting that is richer, more meaningful, and connected to the timeless teachings of Stoicism. Are you ready to embark on this adventure together?

Chapter 1:

Stoicism and Fatherhood

With its unique combination of joys and challenges, fatherhood discovers an unexpected ally in the ancient philosophy of Stoicism. This timeless school of thought, rooted in ancient Greece, provides philosophical guidance for parents seeking wisdom, resilience, and a connection to virtuous living.

In the Stoic approach to parenting, virtue takes center stage: wisdom, courage, justice, and temperance become guiding principles in decision-making. Fathers find themselves navigating the unpredictable journey of parenthood with a moral compass firmly anchored in these virtues.

At the core of Stoicism is the concept of discerning the controllable from the uncontrollable. Parents who practice Stoicism learn to focus their energy on things they can influence, fostering resilience as they navigate the uncertainties of parenthood with a calm recognition of the inevitable twists and turns.

The Stoic dad, guided by the principles of philosophy, navigates the unpredictability of parenthood with a steady hand, drawing strength from the Stoic virtues. Thus, a Stoic father seeks wisdom to guide his children, courage to face the uncertainties of parenthood, justice to instill values, and temperance to balance the joys and challenges of raising a family.

Despite how long it's been around, Stoicism is not a distant philosophy; it is a living philosophy to apply in the present. Parents who embrace Stoicism find practical tools to manage stress, make thoughtful decisions, and foster resilience in their children. The Stoic approach encourages parents to lead by example, demonstrating the virtues they wish to instill in their families.

We will see in this chapter the powerful narrative that emerges from those fathers who navigate the complex seas of parenthood with wisdom, resilience, and an unwavering commitment to a virtuous life.

Stoicism and fatherhood create a profound synergy that enriches the experience of both father and family, demonstrating that ancient wisdom resonates with timeless relevance in modern family life.

Ancient Wisdom: On the Shoulders of the Past

Civilization, in its continued evolution, stands on the shoulders of the thinkers of the past, who weave the fabric of our understanding and shape the foundations of society. These philosophers, visionaries, and sages are the silent architects of our collective destiny, leaving an enduring legacy that nourishes and guides generations to come. Throughout history, we find the teachings of Plato, Aristotle, Confucius, and many others, intertwined with the events that have marked the future of humanity. Each thinker, with his unique and insightful vision, has contributed to the building of civilization, providing the conceptual foundations on which our institutions, values, and social norms are built.

Among these great philosophies of ancient wisdom, one philosophical school stands out as a beacon of resilience and virtue: Stoicism. Rooted in the teachings of philosophers such as Zeno of Citium, Chrysippus, and Epictetus, Stoicism emerged in ancient Greece as a practical guide to dealing with the complexities of life. We will see that its enduring appeal, that quality that has sustained this philosophy through the centuries, lies in its focus on mastering one's mind, cultivating virtue, and embracing a calm acceptance of the inevitable (Británica, 2020).

Reflection on the past then becomes an act of deep connection with our intellectual roots. And for those of us who are parents, it is a very interesting quality to train. Reflecting means navigating between our ideas and the ideas of those who came before us. That path offers a treasure trove of wisdom that illuminates present challenges and shapes the horizon of future possibilities. It is as if, in dialogue with these thinkers of the past, we receive guidance from teachers who transcend time, giving us timeless perspectives.

Reflection is how Zeno lived it, in his dialogues with the dead. For him, "speaking with the dead" was the connection with the philosophers who preceded him and laid the foundations for what would later become Stoic principles. This exchange between past, present, and future proved essential to the evolution of civilization. The thinkers of the past not only offer us insights into eternal questions, but also encourage us to question and reinterpret their ideas as time moves forward and context changes.

In this journey of reflection and construction, we realize that the thinking of the past is not static or rigid; it is dynamic, fluid, and above all, adaptable. Today we can draw on the contributions of philosophers, writers, and scientists from previous times. This is how we honor their legacy and also create a bridge to tomorrow. In this process, we grow, mature, and transform as people and as parents.

Being thoughtful parents and building our path on the shoulders of thinkers becomes an act of humility. We become guardians and continuers of an intellectual tradition that transcends the limits of our own existence. And that's how we teach it to our children. In this intergenerational exchange, the relationship with them is enriched and reinvented, shaping a future that, although unknown, is shaped by the perennial wisdom of those who thought before us.

Basics of Stoicism

In the solid edifice of Stoicism are the fundamental pillars that give identity and substance to this ancient philosophy. By delving into its essential principles, we discover a philosophical ideal that has withstood the passage of centuries, offering valuable guidance for those seeking to live with purpose and serenity. Here we begin our path toward Stoic fatherhood, knowing the founding principles of this set of visions that, two millennia later, remains firm and unwavering.

It is at the heart of Stoic philosophy that we find the central concept of all of this: the dichotomy of control. This notion highlights the importance of clearly discerning between what is within our reach and what is beyond our control. This principle, more than a simple distinction, becomes a compass that guides our actions and urges us to direct our energy toward those spheres where we can make a significant impact.

Have you ever thought deeply about this? About how much you control? Do you worry about things over which you have no control? How much of all that wasted energy could you use in more practical aspects? That's what this principle is about. For us parents, it means optimizing the use of our energy in variables that positively transform our reality and that of our children.

Personally, incorporating this mindset into my life allowed me to relax. Somehow I managed to "let go" of those worries and uncertainties over which I had no control. In this way, by reducing stress levels, I found spaces and energy to channel in the best possible way to my children. Perhaps the clearest example, and one that most parents probably experienced, is checking several times a night if your baby is breathing. A normal situation, natural for every parent, but at the same time limited in terms of your control. You can do everything you can to make sure your baby is well, but there comes a point when they are no longer dependent on you—a point at which, simply, "things happen." We will see later how Stoicism deals with these scenarios.

Furthermore, Stoicism fervently embraces the four cardinal virtues: wisdom, courage, justice, and temperance. These virtues, as ethical cornerstones, provide a solid foundation for informed decision-making and personal growth. Wisdom guides us in the search for knowledge and discernment, courage prompts us to bravely face challenges, justice calls us to act with equity, and temperance invites us to maintain balance in our actions and emotions. But we will look at these concepts in more depth in the next chapter.

Is there a dad who doesn't want his children's lives to be governed by these principles? I mean, they are mostly positive aspects with great benefits for life. We all want wise children who master the art of decision-making and who think before acting. We also want courageous children who feel fear (because it is healthy to feel it) but know how to turn it into novel actions. No one in their right mind can believe that they are not afraid of anything. Having courage does not mean not being afraid, but rather prevailing despite (or because of) their fears.

Likewise, a sense of justice and temperance are fundamental aspects to foster in our children. Taken together, these principles constitute a timeless framework that goes beyond circumstances and times. They enable those who embrace Stoicism to not only face everyday challenges with a clearer perspective, but also to forge a life imbued with purpose and meaning.

Stoicism and Its Deep Influence on History

In the days when togas were fashionable, Stoicism was not just a philosophy; Zeno was pretty much the cool kid on the Roman time. As the Roman Empire flexed its muscles, Stoicism followed, going far beyond its Greek roots. It wasn't just an idea; watching Roman culture, and politics it became a lifestyle. Key players such as Seneca, Epictetus, and Marcus Aurelius influenced Stoicism, making these ideas the most modern thing since gladiator sandals.

Seneca, the philosopher friend of Emperor Nero, not only had lofty ideas; he also gave practical advice on how to be a brave man in the chaotic Roman court. His letters and essays are like the ancient version of tricks for anyone who is interested in Stoicism and lives correctly.

Epictetus then settled in Rome and taught everyone, from senators to ordinary citizens, to control themselves and not let the chaos of life ruffle their metaphorical feathers.

Finally, it was Marcus Aurelius, the Stoic emperor, the rock star. His *Meditations* gives you a behind-the-scenes look at the daily struggles and dreams of a ruler with a Stoic vibe. It's like a crash course in how Stoicism can be your guide to navigating the roller coaster of life. It is important to clarify that this humble and thoughtful man was, in turn, the most powerful man on the planet.

Fast forward to the early Christian era: The appeal of Stoicism was still strong. Early Christian thinkers said, "Hey, this Stoicism thing aligns a little bit with what we're preaching." The focus on being a good person, having self-control, and preaching inner transformation—it all sounded like a Christian song. Seneca and Marcus Aurelius were like those cool guys whose ideas influenced early Christian rock stars like St. Augustine, who, you guessed it, recognized Stoicism in his works (Modern Stoic Man, 2023).

When the Roman Empire dropped the microphone, Stoicism took a backseat. Christianity and other philosophical schools stole the show, and Stoicism took on a retro feel. But the central Stoic ideas didn't disappear: The humanists of the Renaissance sought to recover old philosophical successes. It was in that context that thinkers like Michel de Montaigne and Justus Lipsius brought Stoic vibes to the party, making it cool again.

In the here and now, Stoicism is making a comeback tour. Contemporary rock stars like Albert Ellis, William B. Irvine, and Massimo Pigliucci are improvising on Stoicism, showing a new generation that these old ideas are still a slap in the face. So, if you're a parent looking to add a little Stoic magic to your parenting skills, you're in good company. Stoicism's enduring charm? It's all about its down-to-earth usefulness. In a world filled with challenges and constant distractions, Stoicism isn't some outdated philosophy; it's like your evergreen guide to building smarts, goodness, and that Zen vibe inside you (Modern Stoic Man, 2023).

Stoicism was positioned as an ancient philosophy that endures in the 21st century and manifests itself as a beacon of wisdom in the midst of the complexity of modern life. As we saw, its roots go back to the tumultuous times of the Macedonian empire, when Zeno, facing the aftermath of wars and the loss of all his possessions, forged this philosophical current in Athens more than two millennia ago.

Often misinterpreted as a path of emotional suppression, Stoicism actually embraces a thoughtful management of our emotions. It is not about canceling feelings, but about understanding them and facing them with wisdom. Throughout Stoicism's development, from Athens to Rome, followers of this philosophy faced challenging historical events. And, even with their differences in context, they managed to sustain this set of ideas despite the passage of time.

Unlike the common perception that associates it with austerity and lack of emotion, Stoicism is revealed to be a practical and deeply relevant guide to daily life. Zeno's teachings focus on practical and applicable situations, such as managing anger, confronting insults, and contemplating the fear of death. Following in the footsteps of Seneca, Stoics advocate bravery and honor even in the most difficult situations, adapting these ancient teachings to the pulse of modern life.

Remember: Stoicism does not advocate a lack of emotion, but, rather, conscious control of the mind. This philosophy, like Epicureanism, suggests a focus on personal development and self-discipline. In a world characterized by frenetic capitalism and constant stress, Stoicism is revealed as an indispensable tool. Following the words of Epictetus, we are advised to be selective with the information we consume, while the reflections of Marcus Aurelius urge us to consider our own actions in the face of external rudeness (Dichter, 2017).

The Idea of the Stoic Dad

Parenting becomes an art of mastery when you adopt the Stoic perspective, because at the end of the day, it is up to you to incorporate this knowledge. You have the responsibility to take advantage of this opportunity and positively transform your life. And you hold in your hands the possibility of becoming a better father and human being.

This ancient wisdom becomes a lighthouse in the storm and proposes different mantras that lead you forward on the path of parenthood. But there's no point in knowing about Stoicism if you do not apply the precepts previously presented in your daily life. I learned to accept what I cannot change and, suddenly, I found a peace that I didn't know I needed and didn't know existed. The Stoic virtues became powerful tools that, sometimes unconsciously, I began to use daily.

At the time, when I discovered these practical applications, it felt like a revelation. Stoic parenting becomes a daily practice, and every day I discover strategies for dealing with the unpredictable without losing my cool. One day, my son decides to decorate the walls with crayons, and instead of exploding, I take a deep breath and find a solution without losing my mind.

I know what you might ask: Is it realistic to stay calm in the midst of family chaos? I ask myself this question constantly, but every time I manage to do it, I see how the dynamic at home changes. Nobody says it's easy—in fact, if you think this path will be easy, it may not be the right philosophy for you. There will be challenging moments, where you must overcome your limitations and surprise yourself with how you react to different situations.

Not everything in parenting aligns perfectly with Stoicism. There are times when modernity demands a more adaptive response, but I still find a balance. Stoic philosophy becomes my guide, not a rigid rule. For example, the idea of absolute apathy proposed by classical Stoicism is not a concept that I share, nor that I apply in my life. In fact, as a dad, apathy goes completely against how I want to parent my kids.

How can I completely ignore your feelings for my children? Applying Stoicism to the letter in your life as a dad, at least for me, is impossible.

I hear inspiring stories all the time from other parents who apply these principles and transform challenges into opportunities to grow. And we all have our own "version" of the Stoic dad. A community of parents who, by embracing the Stoic philosophy, discover a more serene and enriching path in the adventure of being a dad. In this way, the idea of the Stoic dad takes shape.

The experience of parenting can take on a unique perspective when explored through the prism of Stoic philosophy. Imagine how Stoicism can become a masterful guide for your parenting, propelling you toward deep personal growth and parenting mastery.

At the heart of Stoicism is the idea that virtue is the highest good. As a parent, by aspiring to Stoic mastery, you will embark on the cultivation of virtues such as wisdom, courage, justice, and temperance. Wisdom will be your ally in making decisions that benefit your children, while courage will give you the strength to face the challenges of parenthood with resilience.

Conscious Parenting

Mindfulness is an activity focused on caring for physical and emotional health. It is a meditation technique to stop, think, feel, and meditate on our actions, to become more aware and live more focused and less stressed. It focuses on the now. In this way, it helps us make decisions calmly, weighing the arguments and respecting and attending to our little ones' needs—without sacrificing our own.

The objective is to consciously pay attention to our thoughts and emotions to detect and identify them, observe them objectively, and thus prevent them from overwhelming us. At the same time, it also allows us to be more aware of what is happening around us. The key to mindfulness is precisely that this internal and external observation must be done from the perspective of a "neutral observer," so that our subjective emotions do not saturate us.

This way we avoid reacting to experiences in "autopilot" mode but, rather, by being present and centered. It helps us focus our attention and live the experience of motherhood/fatherhood with acceptance, serenity, and happiness, taking care of our attitude toward it.

To introduce mindfulness into our daily family life, we must take advantage of the moments of silence we have each day to spend a few minutes listening to ourselves, and thus be aware of how our body and mind are doing. We must consider how we normally respond to our children's demands: on autopilot or consciously?

When putting all this into practice, we can look for those situations in which we must attend to the needs of our little ones and turn them into a good start to transform the daily routine into a moment of connection with them, rather than a habit or feeling like it's mandatory. And one my most favorable moments of connection is the bath, in which the care of my baby's skin is the protagonist.

Resilience in the Face of Challenges

Life is marked by challenges that, although they sometimes seem like imposing blockades, are transformed into opportunities to grow and flourish. This experience shows us how resistance emerges and transforms into a fundamental virtue for the Stoic father, a beacon that illuminates the path toward personal development and building a deeper connection with his children.

When we immerse ourselves in the daily life of being parents, we find sleepless nights, moments of frustration due to the little ones' tantrums, and the defiant rebellion of teenagers. In these instances, resistance becomes the foundation on which we build the strength necessary to face challenges with patience and determination.

Being a Stoic parent involves more than simply overcoming these challenges; it involves embracing them as an integral part of the parenting journey. Every sleepless night is an opportunity to demonstrate patience and unconditional love. Every tantrum is a lesson in understanding and empathy, reminding us that our children's emotional growth is often a tumultuous process.

When your children grow up, adolescent rebellion (far from being a mere obstacle) becomes fertile ground for building emotional bridges. Here, resilience manifests as the ability to stand firm with love and guidance, offering a beacon of stability in the midst of emotional storms. We understand that these trials are an inherent part of the journey, and it is through resilience that we transform challenges into cornerstones for growth and connection.

By viewing these challenges as opportunities to grow, Stoic parents nurture not only their relationship with their children, but also their own personal development. Each sleepless night, each test of patience, becomes a step on the ladder toward mastery in parenting. Resistance becomes the sap that feeds the tree of fatherhood, allowing it to flourish even in the most difficult terrain.

Thus, resilience becomes part of your life it becomes the bridge between challenge and fulfillment, between adversity and growth. Instead of seeing these moments as pitfalls, Stoic parents see them as opportunities to strengthen the bond with their children and to build a stronger character in themselves.

Father's Teachings

Your role as an educator becomes an opportunity to sow the seeds of resilience and virtue in your children. Instead of simply conveying academic information, you offer them life lessons rooted in bravery and perseverance.

The importance behind this philosophy is to give your children the necessary tools to face challenges with courage and determination. You urge them not to fear obstacles, but to see them as opportunities to grow. Your guidance helps them understand that adversities are an integral part of life and that resilience is the strength that will allow them to get up from falls and learn from each experience.

Honesty, integrity, and kindness are not just abstract concepts for Stoicism, but concrete pillars in building a virtuous life. Your everyday actions, rooted in these values, serve as living lessons, shaping not only the minds, but also the hearts of your children.

Thus, teaching as a Stoic father becomes a dance between the transmission of knowledge and the formation of character. Your influence is not only limited to classrooms or schoolwork, but it permeates every aspect of daily life. Teaching with resilience and virtue means nurturing not only the intellectual mind, but also the soul of your children, guiding them toward a full and meaningful life.

Embrace the Beauty of the Ephemeral

Stoicism, with its emphasis on the transitory nature of all things, invites you to embrace the ephemeral beauty of your children's childhood and adolescence. As a Stoic parent, you not only witness their growth, but you also recognize the transience of each stage of their development.

This acute awareness of temporality prompts you to savor every moment you share with your loved ones. Instead of lamenting the passage of time, you celebrate it as the backdrop that highlights the unique beauty of each moment.

Valuing the present time, from Stoic philosophy, implies recognizing the transience of each moment. Time is a finite resource; each moment is unique and unrepeatable. This keen understanding of temporality instills an urgency in the appreciation of life. Instead of putting off happiness or gratitude, you choose to experience them fully in the now.

Instead of waiting for the next great experience or regretting what has happened, we immerse ourselves in the constant flow of time with acceptance and openness. This approach allows us to live a richer life, seizing every moment as an opportunity to learn, grow, and find meaning.

Embracing the beauty of the ephemeral does not imply nostalgia, but rather a conscious appreciation of the present. This attitude transforms your relationship over time, allowing you to fully enjoy the wonder of witnessing your children's growth and development.

We conclude this chapter having explored the essential foundations of Stoic philosophy and its deep connection to the experience of being a parent. We have discovered how the Stoic virtues intertwine with the complexities and joys of parenthood.

On this journey, we have outlined the figure of the "modern Stoic father," one who embraces Stoic teaching to guide his parenting path. This father not only transmits academic knowledge, but also models fundamental virtues, becoming a beacon of resilience, patience, and love for his children. However, the inevitable question arises about the complete applicability of Stoic ideas to the everyday reality of parenthood.

The idea of being a completely Stoic parent, while inspiring, poses challenges. Life—especially parenting—often places us in situations that challenge our ability to remain calm and collected. We face unpredictable challenges, intense emotions, and moments of vulnerability. The question then arises: Is it realistic to apply 100% of the set of Stoic ideas in raising our children?

In the next stage of our exploration, we delve into the four cardinal virtues of Stoicism: wisdom, courage, justice, and temperance. We will observe how each of these virtues can become a practical guide for the modern father, providing him with valuable tools to face the challenges of fatherhood in a more conscious and virtuous way.

As we continue our journey, we will reflect on how to apply these virtues in specific situations, how to cultivate a Stoic mindset in parenting, and how to find a realistic balance between Stoic ideals and the complexities of everyday parenting.

Let's prepare to delve into the profound teachings of the Stoic virtues and discover how they can illuminate our path in the noble journey of parenting.

Chapter 2:

Become a Virtuous Dad

The virtuous life manifests itself as a fundamental good for every parent, providing a solid foundation for raising children and their journey into adulthood. The four cardinal virtues of Stoicism act as essential pillars that support and guide a man's conduct in his role as a father. The goal of this book is to become a Stoic father for your children—therefore, effort and willingness to change are a key piece to mastering the four virtues.

Using the four virtues, I will present the benefits of becoming a wise parent. In this way, you can incorporate the ability to discern between what is truly important and what is ephemeral. We will see that Stoic wisdom will give you practical knowledge that goes beyond pure intellect. Adult life—especially that of parents—is an eternal symphony of decision-making based on an understanding of long-term consequences. A Stoic father will be able to face the challenges of parenthood and lead with insight, modeling a path of authenticity and discernment for his children.

We will also see the importance of being a brave father. The courage proposed by Stoic philosophy is not only related to physical dangers, but it also involves facing emotional and moral adversity with determination. Virtuous parenting will require the courage to face the uncertainties of parenting, admit mistakes, and stand up for what is ethical. The goal is to become a constant source of strength and support, inspiring your children to face life with integrity and courage.

When we talk about justice, the Stoic concept goes beyond legal equity. It involves treating others with kindness and respect. In a father's life, it means creating a harmonious and equitable family environment, encouraging open communication, and considering the needs of each family member. A just father establishes solid foundations for the ethical formation of his children and models lasting behaviors.

Temperance offers the father the ability to exercise self-control and moderation in all facets of his life. In parenting, it involves managing emotions, avoiding impulsive reactions, and maintaining a balance between pleasures and challenges. A Stoic father, being temperate, transmits to his children a valuable lesson about the importance of self-discipline, patience, and resistance in the face of life's vicissitudes.

Throughout this chapter, we will see that the virtuous life gives the father the opportunity to be not only a provider, but a moral guide and a model of virtue for his children. We are talking about adopting Stoic virtues as fundamental pillars, and in this way enriching your existence. Virtue leaves a powerful imprint on the ethical formation of future generations. On this journey toward a virtuous life, the father discovers that his example and legacy transcend the mere act of raising children, becoming the construction of a solid foundation for a more ethical and resilient society.

The Virtues of Stoicism

The Stoic vibe has been a huge eye-opener for me in terms of how to deal with life and all its complications. In this system, physical and thought movements are super connected with an ethical purpose that points directly to calmness, self-sufficiency, and apathy. In other words, it's cool to seek total tranquility, be self-sufficient, and be in Zen mode in the face of life's ups and downs. Those goals have been like my GPS in the search for a life worth living.

The connection between the four top virtues of Stoicism and how you manage in life is no coincidence. The thing about being a Stoic sage, like having complete virtue, shows that real happiness lies in understanding and living in sync with a kind of "universal law" that embraces human nature and the order of the universe.

The move of "living according to nature" is not just following your most basic instincts; it is responding to that logic that is felt in the universe and in yourself. This ethical call is like a mix between what you want and what you have to do. The Stoic theory of "impulse" made me see how this rational response is the very essence of being human.

The way the Stoics see nature, as part of reason and order, completely pivots how I see things. It is not just a meaningless force, but rather a divine wave that permeates everything from nature to our existence.

Human actions, according to the Stoics, are divided into good actions (virtuous), bad actions (vicious). Realizing that Stoic ethics is not only avoiding evil, but also doing good things in line with nature, put me in full ethical responsibility mode. The concept of duty, when achieved in harmony with nature, adds that ethical touch to my daily life, helping me grow morally and responsibly (Quora, 2020).

Wisdom

Wisdom within the Stoic framework goes beyond the acquisition of knowledge; it involves applying that knowledge practically in daily life. For a virtuous parent, this translates into the ability to make informed decisions that benefit the family. This involves not only considering the immediate impact, but also being aware of the long-term consequences of actions. Additionally, it involves having a deep understanding of your children's developmental needs and being committed to continued personal growth. Wisdom, in this context, manifests itself in the ability to guide and lead with insight, contributing to the overall well-being of the family.

Courage

Parenthood, with all its challenges and responsibilities, requires courage. A virtuous parent faces the uncertainties inherent in parenting with courage. This involves making difficult decisions, being emotionally present for your children, and facing head-on challenges that may arise. Stoic courage is not only limited to facing the difficult aspects of parenting, but also to admitting mistakes when necessary. Likewise, it encourages us to firmly defend what is morally correct, thus modeling resilience and integrity for our children.

Justice

In the Stoic context, justice goes beyond the application of laws; it is about treating others with kindness and respect. A virtuous father practices justice by creating a family environment wherein harmony and support reign. This involves encouraging open and honest communication, addressing conflicts with empathy, and ensuring that the needs and opinions of each family member are taken into account. Justice in Stoic parenting seeks to establish a fair and equitable family dynamic, where everyone feels valued and understood.

Temperance

Temperance, a central virtue in Stoicism, is essential for a virtuous father. It translates into self-control and moderation in all facets of life. In the context of parenting, this involves managing emotions and not getting carried away by impulsive reactions, thus maintaining emotional balance. Temperance helps parents stay calm during stressful situations, make thoughtful decisions, and model emotional resilience for their children. Furthermore, practicing moderation in pleasure and difficulties teaches children the value of self-discipline and the ability to face challenges with serenity.

Wisdom and Fatherhood in Stoic Philosophy

Wisdom is, without a doubt, a fundamental virtue that extends far beyond the mere accumulation of knowledge to encompass its practical application in daily life. When we delve deeper into the intersection of wisdom and parenting within this philosophical framework, a rich tapestry of principles emerges.

To begin with, for a Stoic parent, wisdom is revealed in the ability to make informed decisions that contribute to the overall well-being of the family. This goes beyond immediate considerations and involves keen anticipation of the long-term consequences of actions. It is a thoughtful and intentional approach to decision-making, considering how choices impact family harmony and prosperity.

Being a thoughtful parent is an ongoing challenge that involves a deep awareness of my actions and their impact on my children. This constant reflection becomes an inner journey in which I face significant challenges but also experience substantial personal growth.

I remember my two kids were engrossed in their own worlds of homework and play. As I sat there, I couldn't help but reflect on the ups and downs of the day.

In that moment, a memory from my own childhood surfaced. I vividly recalled just a simple incident where my dad didn't pay attention to me. It struck me in that moment that my actions as a parent could have a similar effect on my children.

I began to pay closer attention to them. I learn how to choose the words and the tone I used with them. There started for me a journey of self-reflection. I saw for the first time my thoughts and emotions as a dad.

Starting that day, I found myself better attuned to my children's needs and emotions, witnessed positive changes not only in my relationship with them but also in my own personal growth.

I think the lesson learned was clear: Being a thoughtful parent is not just a responsibility; it's a transformative inner journey that shapes both the parent and the child.

My father was the authority to me, and one of my biggest challenges lies in the need to balance authority with empathy. Reflection leads me to question my disciplinary approach and seek methods that foster understanding rather than simply imposing rules. It is about understanding that effective authority does not always translate into rigidity, but rather the ability to guide with sensitivity.

Therefore, wisdom, understood Stoically, involves a deep understanding of the developmental needs of children. A virtuous parent recognizes that each child is on a unique journey of growth, and wisdom guides them by providing personalized support, guidance, and opportunities for their individual development. This understanding forms a more deliberate and considered approach to parenting.

Wisdom is fundamentally intertwined with a commitment to continuous personal growth. A Stoic father recognizes that his own development directly influences his ability to guide and raise his children. This commitment involves continuous self-reflection, learning from experiences, and cultivating virtues that positively impact personal and family well-being.

Wisdom also manifests itself in leading with insight. The Stoic father serves as a guiding force for the family, offering not only direction but also thoughtful and insightful guidance. This leadership is characterized by a deep understanding of the family's values, goals, and broader context of life.

Emotional resilience, an important Stoic virtue, is inherent in a wise parent. Model a father's ability to manage his emotions, demonstrating to his children the importance of facing challenges with equanimity, resilience, and a clear mind. This, in turn, fosters emotional intelligence within the family.

Central to a Stoic parent's approach is the cultivation of a Stoic mindset. This involves accepting challenges as opportunities for growth and maintaining a calm and rational approach in the face of life's inevitable adversities. This mindset not only influences the father's well-being, but also sets a powerful example for children, teaching them how to navigate life's complexities with wisdom and composure.

Brave Dads, Stoic Dads

Courage lies at the core of Stoicism and, when applied to fatherhood, transforms dads into resilient and brave figures. Beyond mere physical bravery, Stoicism teaches us that true bravery involves facing life's uncertainties with a calm, rational mind. A Stoic father embraces the uncertainties of parenthood with courage, navigating the challenges of a rapidly changing world and facing the unpredictability of a child's development with a steady mind. This means being prepared to adapt to unexpected situations and find strength in the face of the unknown.

Parenting often requires difficult decisions, from disciplining a child to deciding on their education. A courageous parent, influenced by Stoic principles, approaches decision-making rationally and with a focus on what is morally right. This involves the courage to make decisions that may be difficult in the short term but that align with virtuous long-term goals for the family.

When applied to parenting, Stoicism does not suppress emotions. As we mentioned in the introduction, being a dad and achieving apathy does not make any sense. Apathy, in the classic Stoic view, becomes an invaluable resource for facing the vicissitudes of life. It does not mean callous indifference, but rather a balanced and reasoned response to external events. It is the recognition that, although we may not have control over many situations, we always have control over how we choose to react to them. However, in my opinion and experience, being a dad automatically nullifies this concept.

However, the Stoic dad encourages recognizing and managing emotions effectively. A brave parent in the Stoic sense is not afraid to show vulnerability, express love, admit mistakes, and encourage open communication within the family. It takes courage to be emotionally available and transparent, and Stoicism provides a framework to do so with resilience.

Life and parenting are full of challenges; a brave parent does not crumble in the face of difficulties, but, rather, uses challenges as opportunities for growth. This Stoic resilience helps create a stable and supportive environment for the family. Stoicism emphasizes living according to moral principles. Therefore, this set of ideas invites you to stand firm in defending moral integrity, both in your personal life and in the way you guide your children. This may involve taking a principled stance on ethical issues, teaching children the value of honesty, and demonstrating a commitment to justice and fairness.

Justice and Parental Responsibility

Where justice and parenting are concerned, the philosophy of Stoicism provides valuable insights into how people can approach the responsibilities of raising children with virtue and moral integrity.

For Stoics, being a "just" parent involves fulfilling parental responsibilities in a way that is in harmony with the fundamental virtues of Stoicism. By this, I mean that you must be a dad who preaches from the most natural aspects of being, who lives in the present and also who takes advantage of every moment. In the context of parenting, justice relates to the duty to act equitably and correctly toward one's children. Being a fair dad means having the ability to impose authority over your children, when necessary, but also knowing how to lower your gaze and accept a reprimand, if necessary. In this concept, justice and humility follow similar paths.

As we said, the emphasis on living in accordance with nature and reason guides parents to approach their roles with a sense of justice. As human beings, balance with nature requires us to meet some demands, and when we also become parents, these demands multiply. We talk about responsibilities inherent to the experience of creating life. This includes meeting our children's material needs, fostering their emotional well-being, and providing moral guidance. Stoic parents strive to treat each child fairly, recognizing their individual needs and fostering a warm and kind environment with the upbringing of their children.

Parents, as primary influencers in a child's life, have the opportunity to model virtuous behavior. Stoicism emphasizes the importance of leading by example. Stoic parents are aware that their behavior serves as a model for their children's understanding of justice and ethical conduct. In fact, only after becoming a father did I understand many situations that I experienced with my own father and that, until that moment, had perhaps gone unnoticed.

Has this happened to you? To experience something as a dad and have your brain instantly connect that experience to a memory from your childhood? I mean, those moments when you think, *Ah, now I understand what my father meant by this.* Moments when you think, *Okay, I understand why my father acted that way.* It is a way of proving our parents right for the simple fact of empathy from experiencing similar things, but decades later.

In that constant transformation that parenthood implies, when we talk about empathy, we are also talking about balance. Stoic justice in parenting involves our ability to find a balance between authority and empathy. Stoic parents recognize the need for discipline and guidance while empathizing with their children's perspectives.

However, I correct myself here, as it is not so much "finding" balance as "forging" it. This fair measure, typical of empathic authority, is worked on and incorporated into life gradually. You may already have it innate, as there are people with a more acute sense of justice. There are parents for whom the balance of this variable comes naturally. Well, that's not my case. I found myself struggling in the first part of my experience as a dad. I loved every second of it, but it didn't come easy.

Stoicism teaches people to accept what is beyond their control and adapt to changing circumstances. In parenthood, unforeseen challenges are inevitable. As a Stoic parent I found myself in the position of having to approach these challenges with a rational mindset, adapting parenting strategies to best meet the needs of my children. This adaptability aligns with the Stoic principle of focusing on what you can control and accepting what you cannot control.

Finding balance as a dad was, for me, a great challenge. It took me a few years to understand that I should be a little more flexible and learn to adapt to the individualities and differences of my children. Stoic justice involves treating each person according to their individual merits and needs. Stoics recognize the need for discipline, but it must be applied with justice and empathy. Fair discipline involves imposing consequences in a proportionate and educational manner, seeking the well-being and development of the child rather than arbitrary or punitive punishments. Empathy here involves understanding the child's circumstances and perspectives.

It was hard work; for years I made conscious decisions to "not act" as I would have done had I not given it any thought. For me, balancing was a little counter-intuitive. At the end of the day, this balanced approach allows children to develop a sense of justice, understanding the consequences of their actions and the importance of treating others with fairness and respect.

Resilience is a Stoic virtue, and being a fair parent involves accepting the challenges inherent in parenting calmly and resiliently. Problems and difficulties are inevitable, but a fair father approaches these situations with serenity, adapting to the circumstances and making decisions based on reason. The Stoics emphasize the importance of living according to the principles they've been taught. Thus, a righteous father practices what he preaches, serving as a living example of ethical and moralistic behavior for his children.

Dad's Temperance and Balance

In the practice of moderation, self-control, and maintaining emotional balance, the virtue of temperance occupies a central place. When it comes to parenting, the Stoic principle of temperance is particularly relevant, emphasizing the importance of a calm and balanced approach to parenting.

It is taught that one should not get carried away by extreme emotions. A Stoic father, guided by the virtue of temperance, learns to regulate his emotions effectively. I'm not talking about being perfect or aiming for apathy: Simply becoming more effective is enough for Stoicism. This involves not reacting impulsively to challenging situations, but, rather, taking a moment to reflect and respond in a measured and thoughtful manner. Always remember that the first reaction is the most primitive, and it can—and maybe should—be contained.

To do this we must cultivate patience. (Yes, I told you it was not going to be an easy path.) I don't think I need to explain to you what "patience" is. If you are a dad, it is a concept that you know from the first moment you became a dad and it accompanies you every day for your entire life. In this case, a Stoic parent aspires to understand that children, like all people, are prone to making mistakes. Children seem to be made to test your limits. Stoic temperance, in this context, reduces parental frustration when your children disobey you, because you already know that they will—and you tolerate it.

Patience allows you to guide your children with a firm but fair hand, fostering an environment of understanding and growth. You can assert compassion and set boundaries, but you do so with an empathetic understanding of your children's perspectives.

The influence of a calm and temperate father on his children is profound. Children often model their behavior after their father figures, and a father who exemplifies emotional balance becomes a source of stability in their lives. The calm demeanor of a Stoic father teaches valuable lessons about how to handle adversity, make wise decisions, and face life's challenges with resilience.

Stoic philosophy emphasizes self-reflection. A temperate parent takes time to reflect on his reactions and responses to various parenting situations. This reflective practice allows him to identify areas of personal growth and ensures that his actions align with Stoic virtues. By understanding where he can improve, a father becomes a more effective and balanced guide for his children.

In keeping with Stoic principles, temperance teaches your children the art of resilience. Life is full of ups and downs, and a Stoic approach involves acknowledging setbacks without losing your composure. Your mettle imparts a valuable life skill to your children: It gives them one more tool to navigate the complexities of the world with strength and grace.

Day-to-Day Stoic Strategies for Parents

Dinner Time

Imagine this everyday scenario: Dinner time is approaching, and the kitchen is filled with noise and activity. Kids are hungry, they crave attention, and chores are piling up. Instead of giving in to stress and haste, you decide to practice mindfulness. Stop for a moment before you start preparing dinner. Observe the colors and textures of the ingredients; feel the weight of the utensils in your hands and enjoy the aroma that develops in the kitchen. By doing so, you not only connect with the present, but you also transform a routine task into a moment of calm and gratitude.

Bath Time

Bath time is often seen as just another task on the daily to-do list. However, turn this moment into an opportunity to practice mindfulness. As you help your children bathe, instead of letting your mind wander to the worries of the day or pending tasks, immerse yourself in the present. Feel the warm water, watch your children's laughter and joy, and allow this time to become a calm space where mindfulness replaces the rush. This practice will not only transform bath time into a meaningful experience, but it will also strengthen your connection with your children.

The Conversation With Adolescents

In the context of adolescent children, the strategy could be applied during family conversations. Instead of just superficial listening, practice active, conscious listening. Connect with their facial expressions, observe their body language, and pick up on underlying emotions. Instead of rushing to offer solutions or advice, allow the space to be filled with your attentive presence. This will not only strengthen communication, but it will also foster an environment in which your children feel heard and understood, thus establishing a solid foundation for the relationship.

In this chapter, we have explored the four Stoic virtues—wisdom, courage, justice, and temperance—and analyzed how each of them is deeply intertwined with the experience of being a parent. Parenthood, far from being a simple task, is presented as a challenge that demands the constant application of these virtues to face situations with serenity and wisdom.

It is evident that knowing the Stoic virtues is only the first step. True transformation occurs when we decide to actively incorporate these virtues into our daily lives with our children. Forging a Stoic mindset involves not only understanding the virtues, but also committing to applying them consistently in parenting. The wisdom to understand the needs of our children, the courage to face the challenges of parenthood, justice to balance discipline and affection, and temperance to remain calm in the midst of chaos—all these virtues are essential for parenting.

It is crucial to recognize that none of our parents may have perfectly fulfilled all of these virtues. They may have had some more developed virtues than others, but this does not invalidate their effort or the importance of learning from their experiences. Understanding and forgiveness of our parents' imperfections allows us to move forward with humility and determination on our own journey as Stoic parents.

Looking ahead, the next chapter will explore the importance of acceptance and adaptability in Stoic parenting. Facing inevitable uncertainties and changes with an open and resilient mind is essential to building solid and enriching relationships with our children. As we continue our journey in Stoic parenting, let us remember that each day is an opportunity to apply these virtues and grow both as parents and as individuals.

Chapter 3:

Stoic Rearing—Acceptance and Adaptability

This chapter, dedicated to acceptance and adaptability, unfolds as a fundamental and enriching exploration of everything it means to become a Stoic dad. Within Stoicism, there is an inherent wisdom that invites parents to grapple with the unpredictable and ever-changing landscape of parenting. You know it well. Although life as a dad sometimes seems like a constant loop repeating itself over and over again, the truth is that our children are an ocean of possibilities. Therefore, most of the time, you will have to adapt to them—not the other way around.

This chapter delves into the profound meaning of adopting the principles of acceptance and adaptability to shape not only the dynamics of the relationship between parents and children, but also to create resilient, compassionate, and virtuous individuals. We will see that acceptance, as espoused by Stoicism, transcends mere acquiescence to fate; rather, it is an active acceptance of the present moment, a conscious choice to face the realities of parenthood with a calm and collected spirit.

We will learn to understand the liberating power that comes from recognizing the limitations of control, recognizing that certain aspects of the parenting process are subject to the whims of circumstances. God, luck, destiny...call it what you want: Whether we face unexpected challenges, the unique qualities of each child, or the inevitable uncertainties of life, the practice of acceptance becomes the cornerstone of mental strength.

The Stoic father, armed with the wisdom of acceptance, becomes a beacon of resilience and equanimity for his children. This mindful approach serves as a powerful lesson, teaching the next generation that while external circumstances may be beyond their control, they possess the ability to choose their responses—a lesson that resonates far beyond the realm of parenting. At the end of the day, one of the most fundamental precepts of Stoicism has to do with this: understanding that you don't control what happens, but you can control how you react to it.

Adaptability emerges as a dynamic force that complements acceptance, inviting parents to flexibly navigate the changing landscape of parenting. Each child is a unique individual, possessing different strengths, weaknesses, and temperaments. And, as parents, it is our duty (and one of our great challenges) to learn "the rank" of our children to the letter. Stoic parenting encourages parents to discard rigid expectations in favor of a more fluid and responsive approach. This adaptability allows parents to adapt their guidance to the specific needs of each child, fostering a harmonious and nurturing environment.

Furthermore, as a Stoic parent, you recognize that acceptance and adaptability extend beyond the microcosm of the family unit. The broader social and cultural context becomes a canvas for imparting values of social responsibility, empathy, and understanding of diverse perspectives. We are no longer just talking about indoors, but also about worshiping adaptability with others, so that they can navigate the complexities of a constantly changing world with a firm commitment to virtue.

You will see that the perfect fusion of acceptance and adaptability creates a narrative of resilience, wisdom, and growth. As we delve deeper into the heart of these Stoic principles, we equip ourselves and our children with the invaluable tools necessary to navigate life's unpredictable currents with grace, resilience, and an unwavering dedication to the pursuit of virtue.

Acceptance in Stoic Fatherhood

Parenting in the Stoic philosophy has a crucial commitment to acceptance, a principle that, although essential, proves to be a significant challenge in daily practice. Teaching children the ability to accept life's vicissitudes becomes a monumental task, often characterized by situations in which parents find themselves powerless in the face of circumstances they wish they could alter.

The Stoic notion of accepting what is beyond our control takes on vital relevance in the parenting context. Although philosophy suggests flowing with the currents of life, parents face countless moments when reality seems to defy this principle. The understanding that certain aspects are beyond direct parental control, and the subsequent need to accept this reality, constitutes a complex lesson for both parents and children.

Likewise, acceptance of the uniqueness of each child, a pillar of Stoic parenting, entails a constant recognition of individual differences. This process, although essential for the healthy development of children, can create tension and require deep patience and understanding on the parents' part.

In terms of resilience, the central component of acceptance in the Stoic context, parents face the paradox of wanting to protect their children from adversity while teaching them how to cope with it. The difficulty lies in finding the balance between providing support and allowing children to experience life's inevitable difficulties, accepting that these experiences will contribute to their growth.

The challenge of acceptance in parenthood is intensified in times of adversity, when parents are confronted with unexpected or painful situations. In these moments, acceptance is presented as a virtue that requires significant emotional strength to process and assimilate the complexities of the situation.

Despite these difficulties, Stoic parenting suggests that acceptance does not imply resignation, but rather a conscious adaptation to circumstances. It is a process of continuous development, a discipline that requires constant introspection and a deep commitment to the well-being of your children.

Stoic Fatherhood Challenges

Parenting comes with significant challenges that evolve and become more complex as children go through various stages of development. For example, during childhood, parents face the task of establishing a solid foundation for their children's emotional and cognitive growth. One of the primary challenges lies in balancing setting limits with promoting autonomy, a delicate act that requires a deep understanding of each child's individual needs.

As children enter adolescence, parenthood takes on a different dimension, marked by the exploration of identity and the search for independence. Effective communication becomes a key challenge as teenagers seek to assert their voice and express their opinions. Parents' ability to listen sympathetically and provide guidance without imposing becomes a crucial aspect of family dynamics.

Time and attention management, particularly in today's digital age, also emerges as a relevant challenge. Childhood parenting involves creating a nurturing and stimulating environment, but finding the right balance between time spent on work, family, and other obligations can be a constant challenge.

During adolescence, when rebellion is present in the most basic interactions with your children, proper conflict management becomes a necessity for every dad. As children seek to define their own values and beliefs, it is natural for differences of opinion to arise. Parents are faced with the task of fostering an environment wherein the expression of divergent thoughts can occur in a respectful manner, thus promoting healthy growth.

We will see throughout the book the importance of finding the balance between autonomy and parental supervision and that it becomes more complex during adolescence. Parents must adapt to new family dynamics, allowing their children to make informed decisions while maintaining a sense of responsibility and security.

Among other complications that adolescence brings to us parents, we can find the social pressure and external influences that our children suffer add additional layers of complexity. Parents face the challenge of guiding their children in decision-making in the face of social pressures, while encouraging the construction of a solid and authentic identity.

Let's look into practical examples and helpful tips that specifically address common hurdles faced by parents on their Stoic parenting path.

Emotional Reactivity

- **Challenge:** Inherent emotional reactions, such as frustration or impatience, pose a significant challenge to the Stoic goal of maintaining calm in the face of adversity.

- **Strategy:** To overcome this challenge, introducing mindfulness techniques becomes imperative. Practices like deep breathing allow parents to respond reflectively rather than react emotionally. This intentional response aligns seamlessly with Stoic ideals and serves as a powerful tool in reinforcing emotional control amid the chaos of parenting.

Inconsistency in Modeling Behavior

- **Challenge:** Inconsistencies in the application of Stoic principles can bewilder children who are keen observers of their parents' actions.

- **Strategy:** The key to addressing this challenge lies in recognizing personal imperfections and consistently modeling Stoic virtues. By openly acknowledging one's flaws and actively showing Stoic principles, parents create an environment wherein children witness an unwavering commitment to these timeless values, fostering understanding and alignment.

Adapting to the Child's Individuality

- **Challenge:** Adapting Stoic parenting to each child's unique needs demands a level of adaptability that can be daunting.

- **Strategy:** Overcoming this challenge involves regular self-reflection and an adaptive approach to Stoic practices. By adjusting parenting methods to suit the individual temperament and requirements of each child, parents ensure a balanced and personalized application of Stoic principles without imposing a rigid structure.

Dealing With External Criticism

- **Challenge:** External judgments or criticisms of Stoic parenting decisions can be a testing ground for a parent's commitment to these principles.

- **Strategy:** The path to overcoming external criticism involves developing a resilient mindset grounded in Stoic teachings. It requires staying true to chosen parenting paths despite external opinions, emphasizing personal convictions over societal pressures. This strategy empowers parents to navigate external critiques with confidence and poise.

Recognizing and addressing these challenges through practical strategies not only strengthens the Stoic foundation in parenting but also fosters an environment where the timeless wisdom of Stoicism can genuinely flourish. Each challenge becomes an opportunity for growth, resilience, and the cultivation of a steadfast commitment to Stoic principles in the intricate tapestry of parenthood.

Balance Between Control and Autonomy in Stoic Parenting

In the infancy stage, a parent who follows Stoic principles approaches the balance between control and autonomy with a delicate mix of direction and freedom. Recognizing that children need structure for their development, the Stoic parent will set clear boundaries and provide a safe, organized environment. This structured environment does not seek to restrict the child's autonomy, but rather to provide a framework in which they can safely explore and learn.

Through this approach, the development of decision-making skills from an early age is encouraged. The Stoic parent encourages his children to make choices within established boundaries, allowing them to learn the consequences of their actions in a controlled and guided manner. This lays the foundation for the growth of autonomy and the ability to take responsibility.

With the arrival of adolescence, the Stoic father adjusts his approach to fit the changing needs of his children. During this crucial phase, when young people seek independence and explore their identity, the balance between supervision and trust becomes more vital than ever.

Rather than imposing restrictive control, the Stoic parent recognizes the importance of allowing adolescents to make informed decisions. He becomes a mentor, providing guidance and support, but allowing his children to experience the responsibilities and consequences of their choices. This approach respects the emerging autonomy of adolescents and provides them with the confidence necessary to face the challenges of this stage of life.

It is crucial for the Stoic parent to maintain open lines of communication, encouraging honest and respectful dialogue. This dialogue allows adolescents to share their thoughts and concerns, creating a space where paternal guidance coexists with the children's growing autonomy.

In both cases, whether their child is in childhood or adolescence, the Stoic parent approaches the balance between control and autonomy with a perspective that values individual development, encourages informed decision-making, and seeks to cultivate a relationship based on mutual trust. This approach, rooted in Stoic principles, aims to nurture not only autonomous children, but also ethical and resilient individuals.

Examples and Practical Exercises

Welcome to the exploration of Stoic parenting, where the enduring wisdom of ancient philosophy converges with the contemporary challenges of nurturing and guiding the next generation. Stoic philosophy, deeply rooted in timeless principles, provides a solid and meaningful framework for parents seeking resilience, wisdom, and tranquility amidst the intricate tapestry of family life.

In the realm of parenting, Stoicism encourages the cultivation of virtues essential for navigating the complexities of raising children. Acceptance becomes a cornerstone, urging parents to embrace the uniqueness of each family member and the inevitable fluctuations of family life. Adaptability follows suit, inviting parents to approach challenges with a flexible mindset, ready to adjust sails when the winds of parenthood shift.

We will illustrate how Stoic acceptance can manifest in everyday situations. For instance, when a child spills a glass of milk or forgets their homework, the Stoic parent responds with understanding, recognizing that imperfections are inherent in the human experience.

As we embark on this journey into Stoic parenting, we delve into practical examples and exercises that bridge the ancient wisdom of Stoicism with the contemporary challenges of raising extraordinary individuals. Together, let's navigate the intricacies of family life with Stoic virtues as our guiding stars, forging a path toward resilient, wise, and harmonious parenthood.

This text delves into practical examples and exercises that illustrate how Stoic principles can be applied to the challenges of parenting. Join us on a journey to the heart of Stoic parenting, where timeless philosophy meets the everyday realities of raising extraordinary people.

Child's Academic Performance

- **Example:** Your child is struggling in a particular subject at school despite putting in an honest effort. As a Stoic father, instead of reacting with frustration or disappointment, you accept the situation and adapt by exploring alternative learning approaches. You might engage with the child's teacher for additional support or introduce creative learning methods to make the subject more accessible.

- **Practical exercise:** Sit down with your child to discuss their challenges in the subject. Brainstorm together about different study techniques or resources that might be helpful. Encourage your child to take an active role in finding a solution, helping them foster a sense of autonomy.

Family Schedule Changes

- **Example:** Unexpected changes in the family schedule disrupt your plans. Instead of reacting negatively, a Stoic father accepts the situation and adapts by reframing it as an opportunity for quality time. You might turn a canceled outing into a spontaneous family game night or a shared cooking experience.

- **Practical exercise:** When faced with an unexpected change in plans, consciously pause before reacting. Consider how you can turn the situation into a positive experience for the family. This practice encourages adaptability and fosters a resilient attitude.

Teenager's Decision-Making

- **Example:** Your teenager expresses a desire to pursue a nontraditional hobby or interest that may not align with your initial expectations. Instead of resisting, a Stoic father accepts the teenager's evolving identity and adapts by engaging in open, nonjudgmental communication. You might seek to understand their passion and explore ways to support their interest.

- **Practical exercise:** Initiate a conversation with your teenager about their interests and aspirations. Practice active listening without immediately imposing your views. This exercise builds a foundation of acceptance and adaptability in navigating the evolving dynamics of parenthood.

Parenting Style Adjustments

- **Example:** As your child grows, you notice the need for adjustments in your parenting approach. Instead of clinging to familiar methods, a Stoic father accepts the evolving needs of the child and adapts by embracing new communication styles, incorporating age-appropriate responsibilities, and fostering greater independence.

- **Practical exercise:** Regularly reflect on your parenting methods and their effectiveness. Identify areas where adjustments might be beneficial for both you and your child.

This self-awareness and willingness to adapt contribute to a more harmonious parent-child relationship.

Family Traditions and Celebrations

- **Example:** Unexpected circumstances prevent the usual family traditions or celebrations from happening. Rather than dwelling on the disappointment, a Stoic father accepts the situation and adapts by creating new, meaningful rituals or finding alternative ways to celebrate. This could include virtual gatherings, handwritten notes, or creating personalized family traditions.

- **Practical exercise:** Encourage your family to brainstorm alternative ways to celebrate special occasions or create new traditions. This exercise not only promotes adaptability but also strengthens family bonds through collaborative problem-solving.

Dads Are More Adaptable Than Before

Life goes on and societies evolve. With them, we parents evolve. Logically, each time period and each historical context demanded different virtues from parents, and we always faced those challenges. Let's take a look at how parenting has changed over the generations and why we're hitting the nail on the head in this century.

First of all, let's forget about those outdated gender roles. Now, we're all on board in sharing the responsibilities of parenting. Let's talk about diversity. Gone are the days when difference was viewed with suspicion. We are now open and accepting all shapes, colors, and sizes. This is not only great for the world, but also for our children's education!

There is no longer this idea that certain things are just Mom's or Dad's job. We are a team! Parents are more immersed in the lives of our children, we share more interests, and we relate more as well. Thus, we forged a bond that has never been so strong in the history of parenthood.

Furthermore, it is key to use technology as our best friend. Do you remember when you had to rely only on your parents' ancestral wisdom? Now, with one click, we have access to blogs, podcasts, and even online parenting communities. Information is at your fingertips, buddy. You can use this resource to connect with your children through video games or various platforms.

We now understand that the emotional well-being of children is as important as feeding them. But so is ours. Therefore, as parents, today we give more importance to how we feel, and we concentrate on developing and strengthening that aspect of our lives.

And how about that focus on personal development? We now realize that to be the best parents, we must first be the best versions of ourselves. Let's grow and evolve together with our children!

Stoic Principles Against Digital Distractions

In the days of modern parenting, the pervasive influence of digital distractions emerges as a contemporary challenge, echoing the Stoic call to navigate life's complexities with wisdom and resilience. The pervasiveness of screens poses a formidable test for parents seeking to maintain meaningful connections with their children in an era dominated by technological allure.

Consider the family dinner table, once a sanctuary for shared moments and conversations. Now, you are faced with the brightness of the screens, disturbing the tranquility of the present moment. Stoic philosophy encourages parents to recognize the impermanence of distractions and focus on the lasting value of genuine connections. By anchoring themselves in the here and now, parents can foster a family environment rooted in Stoic principles.

In the digital realm, the Stoic father confronts the influence of social media, recognizing the potential for unrealistic comparisons and the erosion of genuine connection. Stoicism requires a recognition of external factors beyond our control, along with the courage to guide children through the digital landscape with wisdom and discernment.

Video games, often a source of controversy, become a Stoic exercise in moderation. Stoic parents navigate the fine line between allowing engagement with technology and ensuring that it does not compromise the development of virtues. By fostering a sense of temperance and self-control, Stoic principles guide parents to encourage alternative forms of recreation that align with the pursuit of a balanced and virtuous life.

Even during bedtime routines, Stoicism offers guidance. The soft glow of screens that disrupt sleep patterns becomes an opportunity to practice accepting things that are beyond our control. Stoic parents set firm boundaries and recognize the importance of restful sleep as a cornerstone of overall well-being.

To apply Stoic principles, parents cultivate mindfulness in the use of technology, modeling a disciplined and virtuous approach. Open conversations about the impact of technology align with Stoic ideals of wisdom and understanding. Collaboratively establishing guidelines for screen time reflects Stoic values of justice and shared virtue within the family.

Embracing Stoicism involves intentional moments of digital detox. Designating specific times for technology-free activities aligns with Stoic philosophy by emphasizing the importance of present moment awareness and genuine connections. Stoic parents recognize that peace of mind and resilience come not from avoiding distractions but from navigating them with wisdom and virtue.

In this chapter, we have deeply explored the importance of adopting a Stoic perspective in parenting, focusing on acceptance and adaptability as fundamental pillars. A lot of parenting is about adaptation, whether you're a Stoic or not. Being a dad involves addressing the complexities of parenthood; to do so, the Stoic prism allows you to cultivate acceptance of situations that are beyond your control and develop the ability to adapt to unforeseen circumstances. These are crucial skills for a Stoic parent.

In an effort to give you valuable tools to deal with these challenges, practical tips and exercises designed to be implemented at home have been provided. And at the end of all, that's what it's all about. You need to take control of your experience as a dad and move from idea to action, when necessary. That is why we work by creating a practical guide for those seeking to apply Stoicism in their role as parents. These principles in everyday life can foster an environment of growth and development for both you and your children.

In our next chapter, we will dive into the fascinating world of "Stoicism for Children." We will explain how to teach and apply Stoic principles in a way adapted to children's understanding and development. We will address specific strategies to instill resilience, self-control, and practical wisdom in young people, thus allowing Stoicism to become a valuable tool for facing life's challenges from an early age.

Get ready to discover how we can guide new generations toward a path of mental and emotional strength through Stoic philosophy.

Chapter 4:

Stoicism for Children

"The best way for a seven-year-old to improve the world may be to learn and develop new skills that he can apply to these problems when he is older" –Kelsey Piper

Stoics are famous for insisting that "virtue is the only good" for humans. They consider external things such as health, wealth, and pleasure not to be inherently good or bad, but to have value as "material for virtue to act." In ethical terms, the Stoic tradition, along with Aristotelian ethics, is key in the development of virtue ethics (*What Is Stoicism Philosophy?*, 2023).

Additionally, Stoics argue that certain destructive emotions result from erroneous judgments; they believe that people must cultivate a will that is "in harmony with nature." For them, the true measure of someone's philosophy is not what they say, but how they behave. To lead a good life, one must understand the rules of the natural order, as they believe that everything is rooted in nature.

We are experiencing a renaissance of Stoicism, with influence on entrepreneurs, psychologists, soldiers, and athletes. These thinkers have revived Stoic teachings as a legend that illustrates the choice between easy pleasure and defiant virtue, represented by Hercules.

Stoicism has resurfaced today due to a crisis of systems and values. It focuses on the art of mastering your emotions, internal freedom, and the search for complete happiness. Stoic philosophy, often misunderstood as rigid, is about recognizing, understanding, and acting on principles and values.

Contrary to the perception of indifference, Stoicism does not prevent passion in or for life. Zeno influenced positive psychology and cognitive-behavioral therapies, promoting the management of negative thoughts and the change of rigid beliefs.

The Stoic view includes the constant reminder of the inevitability of death, expressed in the principle *Memento mori*. We will see how some stories illustrate the need to confront the duality of life and death. Stoic principles, such as the acceptance of death, resonate in stories that remind us of the fragility of life and the importance of living fully.

As a dad, I think it is crucial to empower the little ones and make them understand that the world is in their hands. I want them to know that they can solve the problems ahead of them and that there are a lot of people out there working hard to help them learn and grow.

Of course, the fight against climate change is part of this package, and yes, it is something important to keep in mind. But I don't want them to see it as if the world is ending and there is no hope.

Kelsey Piper, a *Vox* journalist, put it brilliantly in a recent article. She suggests changing the way we talk about the climate crisis, especially to prevent young people from feeling overwhelmed by apocalyptic messages. The idea is to convey to them that yes, there are challenges, but there are also many people committed to solving them and building a sustainable future (Zamorano, 2022).

At the end of the day, Stoicism goes beyond telling people to suck it up or quit; It is about seeking virtue, which they called *ataraxia*, a calm state wherein desires and fears no longer dominate you. Simply put, they advocated for a life that wasn't tied to the things society says are super cool, like money or power. Rather, they leaned toward a more austere lifestyle, guided by the motto "not the richest is he who has more, but he who needs less."

How to apply this thought to parenting? Well, we can start by teaching the little ones not to fall into the traps of consumerism that surrounds us.

Virtues for Children

When instilling Stoic virtues in children, it is not just about sharing philosophical concepts; it's about creating an environment and participating in activities that promote the development of these virtues. Here's an expanded look at how we can nurture each Stoic virtue in children.

Fostering wisdom in children involves cultivating a love of reading and exploration through books, documentaries, and educational games that stimulate their curiosity. Additionally, we can promote critical thinking through open-ended questions and discussions on various topics, along with presenting role models that exemplify wisdom and intelligence.

As for courage, it's crucial to support children's participation in challenging activities, whether that's joining a sports team, speaking in front of a group, or trying new hobbies. Share stories of brave characters, both historical and fictional, and teach them that making mistakes is an integral part of learning, contributing to the development of resilience.

To instill justice, it is essential to model it through actions and decisions. Fostering empathy by discussing perspectives and feelings of others and engaging children in volunteer or community-service projects builds a strong sense of social responsibility.

Temperance is taught by emphasizing the importance of a balanced lifestyle, including proper nutrition, exercise, and proper rest. Setting limits on screen time and promoting conscious consumption of entertainment contributes to understanding the concept of delayed gratification and its rewards.

Transcendence is fostered by appreciating nature, spending time outdoors and exploring the environment. Promoting a sense of interconnectedness by discussing the impact of individual actions on the community and the world, as well as practicing mindfulness through meditation and reflection, also plays a critical role.

Resilience is built by providing opportunities for children to face challenges and setbacks, highlighting that mistakes are opportunities to learn. Teaching coping strategies to manage stress and disappointment, and celebrating your efforts, not just your successes, reinforces the importance of the journey.

Practical wisdom is achieved by involving children in decision-making processes, allowing them to weigh options and consider consequences. Encouraging advice-seeking from trusted adults or peers and modeling thoughtful decision-making in everyday life complete this aspect.

For kindness, creating a home culture based on praise and rewarding acts of generosity is essential. Analyzing the impact of small acts of kindness and fostering empathy for the feelings and perspectives of others complements this value.

Integrity is emphasized by highlighting the importance of keeping promises and being honest, even in difficult situations. Analyzing real-life scenarios where integrity played a crucial role and modeling it by admitting mistakes and taking responsibility strengthens this principle.

Finally, cultivating gratitude involves establishing a daily family practice in which everyone shares something they are grateful for. Encouraging the expression of gratitude through notes or acts of kindness and discussing the positive impact of gratitude on mental well-being completes this set of core values.

Incorporating these expanded approaches into daily life creates a holistic environment for cultivating Stoic virtues in children, laying the foundation for their character development and overall well-being.

Surround Your Children With Teachers

We all remember this scene from our childhood: Our parents would have a dinner, or all the relatives would come over for a festive meal. We kids sat at the "kids table"—or, after everyone finished eating, they would say goodbye to us and tell us to go watch a movie. To put on our pajamas and go to bed. It was time for adults to talk, and we weren't allowed any a part of that.

When we become parents, we instinctively repeat this pattern. Now that we are adults, we send our children away so we can talk. On some level, this makes sense; not everything is appropriate for children to listen to. Sometimes it feels good to connect with people our age and level.

But this is a missed opportunity. We could be teaching our children so many Stoic principles. Benjamin Franklin wrote in his autobiography about his childhood and how much he benefited from being included in the "adult" conversation:

> "I remember well that he was frequently visited by prominent people... At his table he liked to have, whenever he could, some sensible friend or neighbor with whom to talk and he always made sure to start some ingenious or useful topic for the discourse, which could lead to improve the minds of his children. In this way he directed our attention to what was good, just and prudent in the conduct of life" (The Autobiography of Benjamin Franklin, 1995).

Seneca's father selected Attalus the Stoic to tutor his son. The most powerful lesson Seneca learned from Attalus was about the desire to improve in practice, in the real world. The purpose of studying philosophy, Seneca learned from his beloved instructor, was "to take with him something good every day: he should return home a healthier man, or on the way to becoming healthier." That's timeless advice that every child can understand and put into practice (Estoicos Club, 2023).

Marcus Aurelius devotes the entire first chapter of his *Meditations* to his "Debts and Lessons"—17 entries reflecting what he has learned from various influential people in his life. We meet Marcus through his human origins: his parents, his grandparents, his great-grandparents, his adoptive father, and his guardians. In the final entry of this chapter, Marcus thanks "The Gods" for all the "people who raised me." "He showed Me clearly and often," Marcus continues, "what it would be like to live" (Estoicos Club, 2023).

Reflections for Kids

If we think of the *Meditations* of Marcus Aurelius but applied it to Stoicism for children, we think of a unique and inspiring journey into the world of ancient wisdom, designed specifically for young minds. Inspired by the timeless philosophy of Marcus Aurelius, this adaptation seeks to introduce Stoicism in a way that resonates with children, offering valuable lessons for their growth and development.

In the spirit of Marcus Aurelius' *Meditations*, this children's version is designed as a series of reflections and teachings designed to instill Stoic virtues from an early age.

Reflection 1: The Wisdom Behind Curiosity

Imagine that you have a magical book that can transport you to distant lands and allow you to meet fascinating characters. Just as Marcus Aurelius learned from wise mentors, we too can gain wisdom by exploring the world around us. Embrace the magic of books, ask questions, and let your curiosity guide you.

Reflection 2: Brave Explorers

All great heroes faced challenges and fears. Be a brave explorer in the adventure of life! Join clubs, try new hobbies, and don't be afraid to talk. Remember, making mistakes is like finding hidden treasures—that's how we learn and grow.

Reflection 3: Heroes of Justice

Close your eyes and picture a world where everyone is treated with kindness and justice. We can be heroes of justice by being kind to others and standing up for what is right. Whether it's sharing toys or helping a friend, small acts of justice make the world a better place.

Reflection 4: The Harmony of Balance

Think of your life as a beautiful melody. Just as a song needs the right balance of notes, our lives also need balance. Eat healthy foods, exercise, and rest well. It's like conducting your own wellness orchestra!

Reflection 5: Friends of Nature

Imagine sitting under a big sage tree and feeling a gentle breeze. Nature is our friend and we must take care of it. Spend time outdoors, explore, and remember that we are all connected, like the branches of a tree.

Reflection 6: Brave Hearts

Have you ever faced a difficult puzzle or a challenging game? Life is full of puzzles, too! Be a brave heart, never give up, and remember that the journey is as important as reaching the destination. Celebrate every step forward.

Reflection 7: Wise Decision-Makers

Imagine having a special compass that helps you make wise decisions. We can make wise decisions by thinking carefully, seeking advice, and considering the feelings of others. Every decision shapes our journey.

Reflection 8: Superpowers of Kindness

Imagine yourself with a cape made of goodness. Kindness is our superpower! Share smiles, help others, and watch your kindness create a ripple effect. You have the power to make the world brighter!

Reflection 9: Champions of Integrity

Close your eyes and picture a shield of honesty and promises—that's integrity! Be a defender of integrity by keeping your word, even when it is difficult. Like a superhero with a shield, stand your ground.

Reflection 10: Magic of Gratitude

Imagine a magical jar that is filled with happiness—that's gratitude! Every day, we add something we are grateful for. Gratitude is like a magic spell that makes our hearts feel warm and happy.

The idea is for young people to embark on a journey of self-discovery and character formation, guided by the wisdom of Marcus Aurelius. Each reflection serves as a springboard that empowers children to navigate life's adventures with courage, kindness, and a heart full of gratitude. Through this idea, the timeless principles of Stoicism become accessible and meaningful to the next generation.

Stoic Integration Into Children's Lives

The ancient philosophy of Stoicism has found renewed relevance as a guiding light for instilling resilience, virtue, and a robust moral foundation in children. Stoic integration into children's lives serves as a powerful and practical approach to empower young minds, equipping them with the wisdom and fortitude needed to navigate life's challenges.

At its core, Stoicism encourages the cultivation of mindful awareness in children. Simple mindfulness exercises and practices become tools for developing emotional intelligence and self-awareness, laying the groundwork for navigating their internal landscapes with poise.

Stoicism teaches children the art of resilience through the embrace of challenges. By introducing age-appropriate obstacles and fostering problem-solving skills, parents help their children view setbacks as opportunities for growth, echoing the Stoic belief in the transformative power of adversity.

Parents incorporate virtues such as justice, courage, and kindness into everyday life, weaving ethical behavior and empathy into the fabric of their children's characters. Engaging narratives about virtuous characters further enhance understanding and emulation of these qualities.

Gratitude, a fundamental aspect of Stoic philosophy, becomes a daily practice in children's lives. Whether through gratitude journals or expressions of thankfulness at family meals, children develop an appreciation for life's simple pleasures and carry a positive outlook.

Parents modeling Stoic behavior wield a profound influence on their children. Demonstrating calmness in challenging situations, acknowledging mistakes, and consistently embodying Stoic virtues create a powerful impact, shaping the worldview of young minds.

Stoic stories and parables tailored to children's understanding become engaging vehicles for conveying Stoic wisdom. These narratives captivate the imagination, making the philosophy accessible and enjoyable.

Incorporating Stoic practices into daily routines seamlessly integrates the philosophy into children's lives. Morning reflections, bedtime affirmations, and family discussions centered around Stoic teachings become natural and consistent aspects of their upbringing.

The integration of Stoicism extends beyond the home to educational settings. Schools and programs adopting Stoic principles in character education provide children with valuable tools for personal development, critical thinking, and emotional resilience.

Fostering a growth mindset aligns with Stoicism's emphasis on continuous learning and improvement. Parents and educators praise effort, perseverance, and a willingness to learn, cultivating a lifelong love for learning.

Meditation and Mindfulness for Children

As a parent, promoting your children's mental and emotional well-being should be a top priority. In a world filled with constant distractions and challenges, instilling a sense of inner calm and resilience becomes crucial. A powerful way to do this is to introduce your children to meditation and mindfulness, enriched with the wisdom of Stoic philosophy.

Mindfulness meditation for kids can be summed up as "the art of engaging fully in the present moment." It involves directing attention to the current experience, whether sensations, sounds, or any other observable aspect. Unlike finding a designated serene space, mindfulness meditation does not require reaching a state of absolute mental emptiness. Instead, it encourages a genuine and compassionate examination of the thoughts and sensations unfolding in the now.

This type of practice does not require a serene sanctuary or a mind devoid of thoughts. It is a practice that invites children to observe carefully and embrace the richness of the present moment. This could involve acknowledging their feelings, tuning into the sounds around them, or simply noticing the world unfolding in real time. There is no need for a specific state of mind or a predetermined level of tranquility;

it is about fostering an authentic and benevolent awareness of your current experience.

Therefore, meditation is essentially about completely immersing yourself in the present, without the pressure of reaching a particular state of mind. The idea is to encourage children to pay genuine attention to what they feel, hear, or experience without judging them. Rather than striving for a quiet mind or seeking a specific meditative environment, the focus is on cultivating a sincere and gentle exploration of the immediate moment.

This practice allows children to develop a greater sense of self-awareness and compassion for their thoughts and feelings while they navigate the ever-changing landscape of their inner world. By practicing this strategy, we are giving children the necessary tools to build confidence, manage stress, and confront uncomfortable or challenging situations. Starting this process early in life offers children a greater opportunity to help them develop resilience and hone their capacity for mindfulness as they mature.

We will see that teaching mindfulness to children also plays a key role in the development of three crucial skills during childhood: the ability to pay attention and remember information, the ability to switch between tasks, and the competence to behave appropriately with others. others. These skills, called *executive functions*, are essential for performing more advanced tasks, such as planning, reasoning, problem-solving, and building positive social relationships.

Explore the Meaning of Meditation

Stoicism invites us to embrace a unique understanding of the present. Its principles, rooted in accepting the current moment, identifying what is within our control, and releasing what is not, offer valuable guidance in raising our children. In this context, meditation emerges as a powerful tool to introduce moments of serenity and calm into the lives of our children, allowing them to disconnect from the chaos of daily routine.

The practice of meditation is presented as an essential strategy in the lives of contemporary children, providing an effective means for them to develop mindfulness. As we incorporate these Stoic principles into parenting, meditation becomes a conduit through which children can learn to embrace inner tranquility.

The starting point is simple but meaningful: Start with short, age-appropriate meditation sessions for children. Invite them to sit comfortably, close their eyes, and direct their attention to their breathing. Explain that during meditation, thoughts can arise and fade, but the key is to observe them without becoming attached.

Encouraging connection to the breath during meditation not only provides children with a tangible focal point; it also teaches them to recognize the ephemeral nature of their thoughts and emotions. As children practice detached observation, they cultivate a valuable skill in managing the constant flow of thoughts without becoming overwhelmed.

Through meditation, children can gradually internalize the fundamental principles of Stoicism, learning to accept the present, discern what they can control, and let go of what is beyond their influence. This practice not only promotes relaxation, but it also becomes a catalyst for developing resilience and the ability to face life with a calm and balanced mind.

Mindfulness for Kids

Beyond formal meditation, instill mindfulness in your children's daily activities. Whether eating, playing, or studying, encourage them to be fully present in the moment. Teach them the Stoic idea of distinguishing between what they can control (their actions and attitudes) and what they cannot (external events and the opinions of others). By doing so, children can learn to respond mindfully to challenges rather than react impulsively.

Stoicism emphasizes resilience in the face of adversity. Share age-appropriate Stoic stories or anecdotes that illustrate the importance of perseverance and maintaining a positive attitude. Talk to your children about how challenges provide opportunities for growth and learning, and how adopting a Stoic mindset can help them navigate life's ups and downs.

Stoicism values gratitude for what we have. Encourage your children to reflect on the positive aspects of their lives. Develop a daily practice where you express gratitude for simple joys, fostering a sense of satisfaction and reducing the desire for excess.

Children learn by example, so incorporate Stoic principles into your own life. Demonstrate calmness in the face of challenges, discuss your own experiences with mindfulness practice, and share how Stoicism has influenced your perspective. Not only does this provide a hands-on model for your children, but it also strengthens the bond between you as a parent and them as students.

Strategies for Parents

Raising our children is a universal challenge that requires internal skills, such as awareness of what is, what is changing, and what really matters in the future. Many parents struggle to achieve this awareness, and this difficulty could be the reason behind the worrying rates of anxiety, stress, and depression shown in sociological research.

In the journey of parenthood, we face a range of universal emotions and concerns. We are overcome with fear for our children's well-being, questioning whether they will be hurt, loved, or affected by unfortunate fates due to treacherous relationships. This uncertainty is intertwined with the frustration and distress we experience when things go wrong or our plans fall apart, defying the expectations we had for them.

At times, we feel overwhelmed when our children's demands exceed our current abilities and resources. This feeling is compounded by the loss of sweet moments that give way to inevitable changes and developments, as well as the need to face the setbacks and failures that are an intrinsic part of our children's growth.

Parenthood also burdens us with the heavy backpack of guilt, whether for imposing barriers, not fulfilling our expectations as parents, or sometimes, causing pain to our loved ones. This feeling is intensified when we find ourselves in situations that challenge our usual tools and guides, throwing us into confusion and leaving us perplexed as to how best to approach them.

These fears, frustrations, feelings of overwhelm, loss, guilt, and confusion are the universal domains that make up the complex struggle of parenting. They are the emotional threads that weave our experiences together, forming the very fabric of our connection to parenting. On this shared journey, we confront these emotions, learn from them, and seek ways to grow alongside our children, growing, together, as a family.

These are the common challenges of parenting, the internal pressures we struggle with and confront, forming the seismic challenge that children present to our daily sanity. In some ways, these pains of parenting are inevitable, and they are the motivation that drives my writing and work with parents.

Establish Calming Routines

Introduce mindfulness in subtle ways by incorporating calming routines into your children's daily lives. You can start with brief, quiet moments before bed, guiding them to close their eyes and focus on their breathing. This routine provides them with a space to relax and disconnect from the daily hustle and bustle. As the routine becomes a habit, children will associate the practice with a pleasant and comforting moment.

Short and Fun Sessions

Adapt the practice of mindfulness to the age of your children through short and playful sessions. Use interactive games that involve mindfulness, such as "sound hunting" or "color breathing." These activities not only capture their interest, but also teach them to be present in the moment. As they experience the fun associated with the practice, they are more likely to adopt it positively into their daily lives.

Model the Practice

Children learn by observing, so model mindfulness practice. Show them how you take mindful moments throughout the day, whether it's enjoying a meal in silence or taking a few minutes to breathe deeply in stressful situations. Seeing that you value mindfulness, your children will be more inclined to follow your example. Additionally, you can share your experiences with them, explaining how practicing mindfulness helps you stay centered and at peace.

In this chapter, we have distilled the fundamental virtues of this timeless philosophy and reflected on the importance of guiding the little ones under the tutelage of great teachers. We have covered how Stoic virtues, such as wisdom, courage, and moderation, can be valuable seeds sown in the fertile soil of the child's mind, fostering strong and resilient emotional growth.

However, we recognize that incorporating these teachings into the lives of children in the 21st century presents its own challenges. The digital age, video games, and social networks compete for our children's attention, creating an environment saturated with constant stimuli. The question we ask ourselves is crucial: Can today's children slow down and connect with activities such as meditation and mindfulness?

The affirmative answer arises not only as a possibility, but as a prevailing necessity. In this challenge, parents play a vital role. The connection between parents and children becomes the necessary bridge to guide children through these practices, showing them that, even in the modern era, there are spaces for calm, reflection, and self-knowledge.

The next chapter will dive into the fundamentals of children's emotional development, exploring how Stoic philosophy can act as a beacon to order their minds and hearts. We will focus on the importance of self-control and regulation of one's feelings as essential tools to face the emotional challenges that life presents. On this continuing journey, we will discover how cultivating a Stoic mindset can be a reliable compass to guide our children toward an emotionally balanced and fulfilling life.

Chapter 5:

Emotion Management in Stoic Parenthood

Stoicism emerges as a guiding philosophy that offers a meaningful approach to emotional management. By incorporating these ideas into everyday life, this philosophy encourages parents to cultivate virtue, resilience, and rationality in the face of the unpredictable journey of raising their children.

We will see in this chapter that at the heart of the Stoic father is the will to grow as a person, and to become a great father to your children. To do that, we explore the basic principles that underpin Stoic parenting.

We will navigate the terrain of parental emotion management, delving into the Stoic practice of distinguishing between the controllable and the uncontrollable. By this I mean that we must first recognize and then understand what we feel. This premise becomes a fundamental aspect of what we seek to achieve here.

In Chapter 4 we saw that, as Stoic parents embrace mindfulness to respond clearly to the ever-changing landscape of parenting, the concept of mindful parenting develops. This strategy is honed by encouraging an intentional, virtue-based approach to raising children.

We also explore the importance of emotional resilience for children, imparting Stoic values that encourage adaptability and courage. Finally, we bring Stoic parenting to the fore in real life, applying these principles to the everyday challenges and joys of family life. Join us on this Stoic journey, where ancient wisdom meets the modern complexities of parenting.

Stoic Dad's Heart

Stoic dad's heart encapsulates a unique perspective on how to navigate the wide spectrum of emotions that fatherhood often entails. Rooted in Stoic philosophy, the Stoic dad seeks to cultivate a heart that stands firm in virtue and resilient in the face of life's emotional ebbs and flows.

At the center of Stoic dad's heart is an unwavering commitment to virtue. Whether he experiences the joys of fatherhood or faces challenges, the Stoic dad anchors his emotions in the Stoic virtues we have already seen and commits to the mission of turning moments of darkness into light. The ultimate goal of every Stoic dad is to shape his responses and decisions as a father.

Stoicism does not advocate emotional suppression but rather the recognition and understanding of emotions. The Stoic dad covers the entire spectrum of feelings and recognizes that both positive and negative emotions are part of the human experience. Whether it is the elation of witnessing a child's milestone or the frustration that accompanies the obstacles of parenthood, the Stoic father faces these emotions with equanimity.

As a key element of Stoic philosophy, the concept of distinguishing between what is under our control and what is not is part of everything that makes us true Stoic dads. The Stoic father applies this principle to his emotional landscape, understanding that external circumstances are often outside of his control.

When we accept this premise, life becomes a little simpler and less stressful. When I first understood this precept, I began to "release" meaningless tensions and worries. Those variables in my life that I did not control, I simply put aside, worrying as little as possible.

In contrast, I focused on making the most of every aspect of life that was in my control. For example, when I changed jobs, I went through a series of interviews until the final decision. Once I finished the last interview, and the decision was not up to me, I knew that it was now out of my control. I had done everything I could and had given my all, and now it was up to them.

This idea also has to do with self-awareness. The Stoic father practices observing his thoughts and emotions without succumbing to impulsive reactions. This attention allows you to respond to situations with intention and rationality, contributing to a more balanced and thoughtful parenting approach.

Challenges in parenting are inevitable, and the Stoic dad sees them as opportunities for growth. Rather than being overwhelmed by difficulties, he approaches them with a mindset of resilience and sees them as opportunities to strengthen his character and develop a deeper understanding of both himself and his role as his father.

Anchoring your life and actions as a dad in virtue allows you to recognize the full spectrum of emotions and forge a path of emotional resilience and wisdom throughout your journey to fatherhood.

Conscious Parenting

Conscious parenting, seen through the lens of Stoic philosophy, becomes a profound approach to raising children with intention, wisdom, and virtue. Stoicism provides a framework that aligns perfectly with the principles of mindful parenting, emphasizing self-awareness, conscious decision-making, and the cultivation of virtuous character.

Mindful parenting encourages parents to approach their roles with intention. Instead of being swayed solely by outside influences or reactive impulses, parents with a Stoic conscience consider the long-term impact of their decisions on both themselves and their children. They strive to make decisions aligned with Stoic virtues, fostering an environment conducive to the development of moral character.

A central element of mindful parenting is the practice of mindful presence: being fully engaged and attentive in the present moment with your children. Stoicism, with its emphasis on mindfulness and awareness, complements this approach. Parents with a Stoic conscience strive to be present, appreciating the nuances of each interaction and actively participating in the parenting process.

Mindful parenting within the Stoic framework involves cultivating emotional resilience. Stoic philosophy teaches parents to recognize and understand their emotions, allowing them to respond to situations rationally rather than reacting impulsively. This emotional regulation becomes a powerful tool when creating a stable and harmonious family environment.

In the Stoic tradition, this strategy involves consistent modeling of Stoic principles. Parents demonstrate the importance of living a life aligned with virtue, making decisions based on reason, and facing challenges with resilience. Children, in turn, learn valuable life lessons by observing and absorbing these Stoic principles in action.

I invite you to adopt conscious parenting under the wing of Stoicism. Let us make decisions with intention, practice conscious presence, prioritize virtue, regulate ourselves emotionally, teach resilience, and be living examples of Stoic principles. Let's build a solid path together for our parenting journey, leaving a meaningful and purposeful mark. Let us take on this challenge and create an environment where our children can flourish with virtuous character and strong emotional resilience. The power is in our hands!

Emotional Resilience for Children

Emotional resilience is a crucial aspect of a child's development, and it plays an important role in their ability to cope with life's challenges, setbacks, and uncertainties. It refers to the ability to recover from adversity, manage stress, and adapt to changing situations in a healthy and constructive way. It's about discovering how lifting your spirits when everything seems out of control and fostering emotional resilience in children is essential to their overall well-being and future success. If life makes you feel very stressed, increasing your emotional resilience is like a superhero move—you can be impervious to all the negative attributes that accompany stress.

As parents, caregivers, and educators, we play a vital role in equipping the younger generation with the essential skills to face and conquer the adversities that life may present. Resilience is posited in Stoic parenting as a dynamic quality that transcends mere toughness; it is the cornerstone of emotional strength. It encompasses the ability not only to withstand the pressures of stress, challenges, trauma, or adversity, but also to recover from these experiences with new strength and wisdom.

Furthermore, resilient children and adolescents exhibit a remarkable variety of qualities that go beyond mere survival. They manifest themselves as individuals who radiate confidence and adopt a positive self-image that serves as a basis for their general well-being. This self-confidence propels them toward the world with a sense of purpose and curiosity, encouraging them to explore the complexities that life has to offer.

As these young, resilient minds navigate their ever-evolving existence, they become not only adaptable but also open to new possibilities. Your resilience serves as a catalyst for curiosity, inspiring you to approach the world with an inquisitive spirit. This innate curiosity, in turn, fosters a continuous cycle of learning and personal development, forming individuals who are not only experts at meeting challenges but who also actively seek to understand and interact with the various facets of their environment.

Some Tips on Resilience

Emotional Literacy

Emotional literacy is not just a skill; it is practically the master key for little ones to navigate the exciting journey of life! It's like teaching them to decipher the mysterious language of their emotions.

"Why am I feeling this?" "What is this feeling called?" Those are the questions you will learn to answer. And believe me, this ability not only helps children understand one another better, but also lays the foundation for managing those emotions like true emotional Jedi masters.

Positive Relationships

We are not just talking about romantic relationships, but about those friendships and family ties that are like the backrest of a roller-coaster chair. You need something solid to hold on to when life takes unexpected turns, right? The same thing happens with children.

Connecting with family, friends, and other caregivers not only provides them with an emotional safety net, but it's also like giving them a VIP pass to explore the world with confidence. These relationships are not only the best friends of resilience, but also the perfect travel companions on this exciting journey called growth.

Problem-Solving Skills

Problems are like riddles, and children are the brilliant minds who will solve them. As Stoic parents, we teach them to break those giant challenges down into smaller pieces, like cutting a pizza to share with their friends.

Why? Because suddenly the problem doesn't seem so overwhelming when you see it in manageable portions. And here comes the fun part: thinking about solutions! It's like a detective game, where you explore all the possible ways to solve the mystery. You can give your children a hand, but don't give them the answers. Allow children to decipher on their own the answers necessary to solve any type of problem.

Effective Communication

Let's talk about how to become masters of gab! We are not just talking about words, but about expressing what you feel and think in a way that is like music to everyone's ears. We teach children to say what they think in an assertive and respectful way.

It's like giving them a superpower to navigate those social situations like true warriors. Imagine that each word is like building bridges to more positive relationships. Communication is the key to opening doors to incredible connections! Children who learn from a young age to communicate effectively will understand how to use words as a fundamental tool in their adulthood.

Foster a Growth Mindset

Stoic parents want children to see mistakes not as stops, but as stations on their journey to knowledge. We explain to them that it is okay to make mistakes; we tell them that error is an important part of the learning process and that it is up to them to transform that frustration into a lesson for the future.

We want them to embrace the idea that learning and growing go hand in hand. Setbacks are not dead ends; they are unexpected turns on the exciting path of discovery. And, like good Stoics, our goal is to control how we react to these unforeseen events. Here, every mistake is another step toward success!

Encourage Perseverance

When we seek to inspire, perhaps perseverance is one of the greatest tools we can give our children. We talk to kids about perseverance, which is like saying "never give up." We tell them stories of people who had challenges but didn't give up, like those movie characters who face monsters but keep going.

We want kids to feel that burning determination inside them, that spark that drives them to keep going, even when things get tough. Because every challenge they overcome is like an epic chapter in their story of resilience and success. They are like heroes in their own movie!

Encourage a Consistent Routine

Imagine the routine as the sheet music of a song that makes each day an exciting symphony. Establishing a predictable routine does not just mean doing the same thing every day, but rather seeks to become a source of security for the little ones. This is especially magnified when your children are infants.

When children know what to expect, they become masters at dealing with daily challenges and the emotions they will feel. It's as if each day is an exciting chapter in their own story, and the routine gives them the script to face whatever comes their way. It allows them to anticipate situations, and, therefore, also to anticipate their reactions.

Identify Your Kids' Signs of Struggle

As Stoic parents, we need to be attentive to signs of struggle or suffering that are evident in our children. We're talking about keeping an eye out for those flashing light signals that indicate something isn't quite right. Changes in behavior, signs of emotional distress...those are the clues. While it is true that you are their parent, and that no one knows your children better than you, you also need to know your limits. You can't solve everything in life! And you can't always do it alone, either. Therefore, if we notice that something is not in tune, we do not hesitate to ask the experts for help.

Who are these experts? Mental health professionals who are in charge of emotions and child development. Because when it comes to the emotional health of children, it is always better to have the best by your side. Spotting the signs early can be crucial to avoiding bigger problems later.

Real-Life Stoic Fatherhood

Today, a growing number of parents are turning to Stoic philosophy to navigate the turbulent waters of emotions and challenges. Stoic parenting emphasizes the importance of emotional resilience, self-discipline, and maintaining a sense of calm amid the chaos of family life.

Narratives of Stoic Fathers

Let's say a couple is juggling demanding careers and the whirlwind of raising three young children. One day, faced with a chaotic home and the stress of deadlines, they decided to apply Stoic principles. Instead of reacting impulsively to the chaos, they paused, took a deep breath, and remembered what they could control. By focusing on their responses rather than external circumstances, they maintained a calm demeanor and approached challenges rationally.

Illustrative Examples

- **Bedtime battles:** Sarah, a Stoic mother, faced nightly battles to get her young son to sleep. Instead of succumbing to frustration, she took the opportunity to practice patience and reframed the situation as an opportunity to bond with her son through storytelling and gentle reassurance.

- **Teenage rebellion:** Mark, in dealing with his teenage daughter's rebellion, practiced Stoic resilience by recognizing that he couldn't control his daughter's choices. Instead of reacting emotionally, he maintained open communication, offering guidance without succumbing to anger or disappointment.

Learned Lessons

Stoic parenting teaches us that while we cannot control all aspects of parenting, we can control our responses. Parents who adopt Stoic practices report improved emotional well-being, reduced stress, and strengthened relationships with their children. The philosophy encourages a focus on values, fostering resilience in the face of inevitable challenges.

Navigating Challenges for Success

Embarking on the path of Stoic parenting is not a seamless journey; it comes with its set of obstacles. Common challenges include external pressures, societal expectations, and the ingrained habit of reacting emotionally, all of which test the commitment of Stoic parents. The allure of immediate results might further complicate the journey you're in.

To overcome these challenges, Stoic parents employ a set of strategic approaches. Mindful reflection stands as a cornerstone, with regular introspection on Stoic principles serving to realign parents with their core values and reinforce the importance of focusing on what is within their control. Community support becomes a crucial pillar, as joining or forming a community of like-minded Stoic parents provides a platform for mutual sharing of experiences, knowledge, and effective strategies, fostering motivation and shared growth.

Gradual implementation emerges as a pragmatic strategy, recognizing that adopting Stoic practices is a transformative journey best accomplished incrementally. This approach acknowledges that personal growth unfolds gradually over time. Flexibility in the application of Stoic principles ensures their relevance in diverse parenting contexts, allowing parents to adapt their practices to varying situations.

Educational resources play a vital role, offering Stoic parents deeper insights into the philosophy. Integrating mindful language and modeling behavior consistent with Stoic values reinforces the implementation of these principles within the family environment.

Finally, celebrating progress serves as a powerful motivator. Stoic parents recognize that the journey is marked by continuous improvement, and each step forward, no matter how small, signifies their child's commitment and growth.

Be a Coherent Dad

Maintaining consistency in Stoic parenting is an enduring journey that demands both unwavering perseverance and a steadfast commitment to self-awareness. Parents embarking on this path must recognize that setbacks are not failures but opportunities for growth, making perseverance a guiding principle. A commitment to self-awareness is central to Stoic parenting, requiring regular introspection to align responses with Stoic principles.

Periodically revisiting Stoic teachings is essential, offering parents the chance to immerse themselves in wisdom and gain fresh insights applicable to their daily challenges. Adjusting expectations to align with the unpredictable nature of parenting, Stoic parents view setbacks as valuable lessons rather than defeats. Community support plays a crucial role, fostering a shared commitment to Stoic principles and providing mutual encouragement.

Consistency is rooted in cultivating Stoic habits, integrating daily rituals inspired by Stoic principles. Adaptability is key, as Stoic parents learn to apply principles flexibly to various parenting contexts—they understand that every parenting journey is different. Embracing the journey, focusing on progress rather than perfection, and understanding that personal growth takes time are paramount for sustaining coherence in Stoic parenting.

To conclude our exploration of emotion management in Stoic parenting, we will review the deep foundations that define the Stoic parent. A central element of Stoic philosophy is the recognition that true strength lies not in the suppression of emotions but in their masterful understanding and management. As dads who embrace Stoicism, it is imperative to embark on an introspective journey, plumbing the depths of our emotions and honing the ability to navigate them with wisdom and virtue.

Understanding and managing our emotions is not simply a personal effort; it is a gift we offer to our families. The Stoic father, endowed with emotional intelligence, becomes the cornerstone of stability in the home. It is about cultivating inner serenity to finally develop a harmonious environment that has a positive impact on the lives of his loved ones, especially his children.

Conscious parenting, a cornerstone of Stoic parenting, underscores the transformative power of validating our children's feelings. Recognizing and empathizing with their emotional experiences allows us to give our children resilience and strength. They learn not to fear emotions, but to navigate them with courage and wisdom, reflecting the Stoic values we embody.

Resilience and Stoicism, once considered niche concepts, have taken on unparalleled value in recent years. In an ever-changing world, the ability to weather the storms of life with composure and resilience is a skill of immeasurable value. The Stoic father, grounded in principles that transcend passing circumstances, models this resilience for his family.

As we move on to the next chapter, dedicated to constructive communication in the family, we carry forward the torch of Stoicism.

Applying the eternal principles of Stoicism is essential to achieving our goal. We're talking about fostering an atmosphere where open and constructive communication thrives. Join us as we explore how Stoic ideals guide us to build connections and foster understanding within our families, creating a foundation of strength and harmony for generations to come.

Chapter 6:

Constructive Communication in the Family

Family life in the 21st century represents a complex network of challenges that have never occurred in families before. The art of constructive communication is an axis to promote understanding and harmony, two concepts that must be conceived as fundamental pillars in the complex communication dynamics of a family.

Stoicism, with its emphasis on reason, virtue, and the pursuit of a calm mind, offers invaluable insights into effective communication within the family unit. A Stoic dad, armed with the wisdom of self-control, strives to communicate not only with words but also with the essence of Stoic principles. A central element of this philosophy is the recognition that one can control reactions and, by extension, the tenor of family discourse.

The Stoic dad, based on the understanding that emotions can be moderated and responses chosen, becomes a beacon of calm within the family dynamic. We talk about practicing reflective communication, fostering an environment where ideas and concerns can be shared openly and respectfully. This aligns with the Stoic ideal of living in accordance with nature, recognizing the interdependence of family members and the collective pursuit of eudaimonia: a flourishing and virtuous life.

If we commit to the premise of applying Stoic principles to family communication, we will see how the same dynamic encourages parents to practice empathetic listening and respond with wisdom rather than impulse. By recognizing the inherent value and dignity of each family member, a Stoic parent fosters an atmosphere wherein different perspectives can coexist harmoniously. Through the lens of Stoicism, conflicts become opportunities for growth and disagreements become paths to deeper understanding.

In this chapter, we delve into practical strategies inspired by Stoic philosophy to improve family communication. From active listening and the art of asking insightful questions to discerning what is within our control, Stoicism serves as a compass that guides parents through the challenges of modern family life.

As we embark on this exploration of constructive communication in the family, we invite parents to integrate Stoic principles into their interactions, recognizing that the path to family peace of mind is paved with deliberate and conscious communication.

This chapter explores how Stoic philosophy, when applied to parenting, can serve as a guide for navigating the complexities of family interactions. Join us to discover the transformative potential that lies in embracing Stoic virtues in the conversations that shape the 21st-century family landscape.

The Importance of Family Communication

Being a Stoic dad comes with its own set of challenges, especially in these times, when the world has transformed into a place where dealing with the whirlwind of technological advancements, changing social norms, and the vast digital realm can make the journey of parenting in the 21st century seem like a complex labyrinth. However, in the midst of these challenges, communication emerges as a powerful tool: a guiding light to help Stoic parents navigate the intricate path of contemporary parenting.

As the world evolves, so do social norms. Stoic parents, rooted in timeless wisdom, understand the importance of open, empathetic communication. Let us engage in conversations that bridge generational gaps, fostering an environment where understanding and respect thrive.

Now, let's delve into the reasons why fostering thoughtful communication within your family is not only essential but can be a transformative force, particularly when you incorporate Stoic principles into your daily life, and especially when lack of communication causes problems in family life.

When you meet to discuss a specific topic, it's like opening a treasure chest of solutions. The magic lies in opening those lines of communication, allowing both parties to express their concerns and find collaborative solutions that benefit everyone involved.

Imagine the beauty that unfolds when you start genuine conversations with your family. By sharing your beliefs and listening to theirs, you are not only paving the way to mutual understanding, but also gaining insight into the "why" behind their actions. Even if disagreements persist, this sharing of perspectives can foster deep mutual appreciation.

Families are a strong support system. Effective communication ensures that everyone is on the same page with their loved ones' needs. Whether offering practical help or simply listening, your family becomes a tightly woven safety net, ready to protect each other during sunny and stormy days.

Family members may not always agree on personal issues—it is during these times that sharing diverse perspectives becomes a valuable gift. While it may be difficult to hear a different point of view, remember that it offers a complete understanding of the situation. Share your thoughts, take a step back, and allow your loved ones the space to consider your perspective.

By nature, family dynamics can be a focus of chatter. Misunderstandings can spread like wildfire. A powerful antidote? Direct communication. Instead of letting misconceptions flourish, approach the family member involved and have an open conversation. It's a sure way to dispel rumors and ensure everyone is on the same page (Hardy, 2023).

To do this, trust, dear Stoic parents, is the glue that unites families. Through open communication, you are not just exchanging words; you are creating an environment of love and understanding. In the midst of life's challenges, a family with a solid communicative foundation becomes a refuge, a place you can always return to for comfort and support.

Modern Challenges for Parents: The Stoic Approach

In the age of social media and digital communication, navigating this landscape requires careful consideration. We guide our children carefully, teaching them the discernment necessary for responsible online participation, and the principles of self-control and conscious use of technology become our allies in helping our children navigate responsibly in the digital world.

However, now more than ever it is important for Stoic parents to approach communication with intention and mindfulness. Let's remember the value of genuine face-to-face interactions within our families, regardless of how much digital noise we have in our homes. It's about instilling a sense of balance that opens up familiar spaces where meaningful connections can flourish.

While the external world may change rapidly, the values of virtue, wisdom, and intentional communication remain Stoic anchors that provide steadiness in the storm. Family communication connects us with the eternal principles that we want to transmit to our children, smoothly overcoming the challenges of digitalized modernity.

Stoic parents not only resist the complexities of modernity but also cultivate a family environment that reflects the enduring essence of Stoicism in the 21st century. Together, let us navigate this journey with empathy, understanding, and commitment to foster connections that stand the test of time.

From the constant bombardment of information to the rapidly changing dynamics of social norms, parents face a unique set of difficulties. In the face of these challenges, taking a Stoic approach offers a resilient, time-tested philosophy to guide parents on their journey. Let's look at some practical tips to consider:

- One of the modern challenges for parents lies in the *incessant flow of information* in the digital age. Stoicism encourages a discerning approach to this information overload, emphasizing the importance of focusing on what is within our control and letting go of what is not. Try to adopt the Stoic principle of understanding the limits of our influence, so you can maintain a sense of calm in the midst of chaos, encouraging a more intentional and purposeful parenting style.

- The *changing landscape* of social norms can also be a source of stress for parents. Stoicism advocates a firm commitment to virtue and reason, providing a stable foundation in the face of changing cultural tides. Align your parenting decisions with timeless principles rather than fleeting trends; then you can navigate the complexities of social expectations with resilience and moral clarity.

- The *fast pace of modern life* can create a feeling of being constantly busy and overwhelming for parents. Stoic philosophy encourages mindfulness and the cultivation of inner tranquility. By adopting practices like mindfulness meditation and intentional reflection, parents can find moments of peace amid the hustle and bustle, fostering emotional resilience and a more balanced approach to family life.

Stoic Strategies for Family Communication

Undoubtedly, the emergence of technology and the omnipresence of social networks have greatly transformed family dynamics, bringing with them both opportunities and challenges. This paradigm shift invites us to reflect on how Stoic philosophy, with its timeless principles, can provide invaluable guidance in navigating these modern challenges and cultivating healthier, more meaningful family communication.

No one can deny that technology has been integrated into virtually every aspect of our lives; therefore, we need to examine how these tools affect our family relationships and how we can use them to our advantage. Stoic philosophy, with its emphasis on self-control and reflection, urges us to be aware of just that. To transform the potentially negative aspects of technology into valuable tools for family communication, we must avoid the pitfalls of constant distraction and work together to foster a fuller presence in family interactions.

For example, social media, while offering instant connections, can also introduce challenges to family communication. Stoic philosophy, with its focus on virtue and reason, suggests that it is crucial to cultivate conscious and authentic communication. By encouraging parents and children to share their experiences openly and honestly, a solid foundation is built for deeper understanding and more meaningful connections.

The ultimate goal of integrating these principles into family life is to transform the challenges of technology into opportunities to strengthen bonds, foster understanding, and create a space where authentic and enriching communication flourishes.

Strategies to Address Distortions in Digital Communication

In the digital world, where nuance can be lost, a key strategy for Stoic parenting is mindfulness. Recognizing potential distortions and striving for clarity and understanding in online interactions reflects the Stoic emphasis on clear, rational thinking. Following are some strategies to help you with this task:

- **Manage screen time and promote family interaction.** Faced with the challenge of excessive screen time, the Stoic strategy is moderation and self-discipline. Stoic parents can consciously manage digital time, creating space for genuine family engagement, thus strengthening bonds and sharing valuable experiences.

- **Cope with stress and improve the quality of communication.** In the face of modern stress, Stoic parenting proposes strategies for emotional resilience and maintaining a calm demeanor. This attitude positively influences the family environment, facilitating more constructive communication aligned with Stoic principles.

- **Prioritize meaningful connections amid lack of time.** Lack of time for meaningful connections can be addressed from a Stoic perspective through prioritization. Checking your daily activities with Stoic values can set aside intentional time for authentic interactions, thereby strengthening family bonds.

- **Navigate generational differences in communication styles.** Faced with generational differences in communication, the Stoic strategy is understanding and empathy. Cultivating an open-minded approach and appreciating diverse perspectives allows for harmonious communication within the family unit, in line with the principles of Stoic parenting.

The Challenges of Stress and Modernity: A Stoic Vision

The environment of modern life places us in front of an undeniable reality: stress has become a constant, aggravated by the incessant demands of technology and social networks. In these times, we are witnessing a strong resurgence of the Neostoic movement. This challenge, intrinsic to our times, invites us to explore the Stoic vision, a philosophy that offers invaluable information on how to address stress and preserve the quality of our family interactions.

Now, the question that arises is this: How can such an ancient philosophy, conceived in such different circumstances—like Stoicism—guide us and provide us with emotional support to overcome the uncertainties we experience today?

Stoic philosophy, in its essence and in the context of modern life, where pressures and demands are incessant, proposes a strategy that gives you control over how and how much what happens to you affects you. This perspective becomes a guiding light. It means recognizing that we cannot always control external events, but we accept them as they occur.

When we talk about stress, Stoic philosophy gives us practical tools to deal with it constructively. It urges us to direct our energy and attention toward those areas of our lives over which we have influence. Rather than succumbing to the anxiety generated by modern demands, Stoic principles encourage us to focus on concrete actions and informed decisions. In other words, don't stress about what didn't happen, because it doesn't exist.

As we saw above, accepting what cannot be changed, a fundamental Stoic principle, frees people from the unnecessary burden of constant worry about events outside their control. This attitude not only relieves mental tension, but also contributes to preserving a calmer, more harmonious family environment.

And if we talk about family relationships, where stress can affect the quality of communication and bonds, the application of Stoic principles takes on even deeper meaning. Stoic philosophy encourages conscious reflection, empathy, and emotional resilience, creating space for mutual understanding and healthy management of collective stress.

Seek wisdom amid the stresses inherent to modern life.

Three Stoic Strategies for Stress

Focus on the Present Moment

In parenthood, especially in a world full of constant distractions and pressures, it's easy to feel overwhelmed by the anticipation of the future or the burdens of the past. It probably occurs to you that time has flown by, and you feel like you didn't enjoy it enough. These feelings generate anguish about the past and, at the end of the day, it is you who has the power to act.

Focus on the here and now. Take a second to think and meditate on what you are experiencing. Sit on the beach and look at the sea, or contemplate the landscape of your city. I, personally, use nature a lot to reconnect with what I consider important. When I feel like I need a moment, or I feel like I'm getting lost in the day to day, I sit on the beach for a while. Sometimes I think deeply about everything, and other times my mind is completely blank.

The important thing is that if the resource helps you relax and focus on the now, use it.

Differentiate Between the Internal and the External

The Stoic distinction between what is within your control and what is not is fundamental. In parenthood, many external events can cause stress, but how you choose to respond to those situations is within your control. Practicing this differentiation allows you to maintain a balanced perspective.

You can influence your reaction, but you can't always control external circumstances. This understanding gives you the ability to deal with stress more calmly and effectively, thus modeling a Stoic attitude for your children.

View Obstacles as Growth Opportunities

Adopting a Stoic mindset that views obstacles as growth opportunities is a powerful strategy for navigating the challenges of parenthood. The Stoics, ancient philosophers who emphasized self-control, virtue, and resilience, provide valuable insights into coping with the inevitable stresses that come with raising children.

Stoicism encourages individuals to recognize that challenges are an integral part of life, and it is our response to them that shapes our character and inner strength. Applying this philosophy to parenthood involves a fundamental shift in perspective. Rather than perceiving stress as solely negative, one can choose to see it as a pathway to personal and parental development.

This Stoic approach involves cultivating resilience, the ability to bounce back from adversity, and viewing each challenge as a learning opportunity. Much like a whetstone that sharpens a blade, challenges can refine your character and parenting skills. Every difficult situation becomes a chance for personal growth, allowing you to acquire new insights, skills, and coping mechanisms. This shift in perspective not only mitigates the negative impact of stress on emotional well-being, but also transforms it into a constructive force for personal evolution.

Stoic resilience equips parents with the tools to adapt to difficult situations effectively. It involves maintaining emotional balance in the face of challenges, which is not only beneficial for the individual parent but also for the overall family dynamic. When parents can navigate stress with composure, it sets a positive example for their children and contributes to a healthier family environment.

In essence, the Stoic strategy of viewing obstacles as growth opportunities empowers parents to approach the trials of parenthood with a constructive mindset. This way, individuals can not only weather the storms of parenting more effectively, but also emerge from them with greater wisdom, strength, and resilience. This philosophy fosters a positive cycle of continual growth and adaptation, enhancing the well-being of both parents and children alike.

Interactive Communication

While Stoic philosophy is often associated with personal resilience and mental toughness, its principles can also be applied to the realm of interactive communication. Stoicism, with its emphasis on rationality, virtue, and self-control, offers valuable insights for fostering meaningful and effective exchanges in various interpersonal contexts.

A key aspect of Stoicism is the idea of focusing on what is within our control and accepting what is not. Applying this to interactive communication means recognizing that we cannot control how others respond or behave, but we can control our reactions and expressions. This principle invites people to approach conversations with a sense of calm and detachment, allowing for more thoughtful and measured responses. The more thoughtful and measured the communication, the greater the possibility of open and constructive dialogue, fostering connection and mutual respect.

The Stoic concept of *logos,* which refers to the divine reason that governs the universe, can be interpreted in communication as the underlying logic or reason in discussions. Adopting this premise encourages people to engage in conversations focusing on reason and logic rather than being carried away solely by emotions. This rational approach can lead to more consistent and effective communication, minimizing misunderstandings and conflicts.

Stoicism's emphasis on self-reflection also plays a crucial role in interactive communication. Periodically examining one's communication style, recognizing areas for improvement, and striving to communicate virtuously can lead to more positive and harmonious relationships. This self-awareness contributes to the development of effective communication skills over time.

Conflict and Stoic Fatherhood: Navigating Challenges With Wisdom

Conflict is an inevitable part of fatherhood, starting in the early years of infancy straight into the tumultuous period of adolescence—and beyond. Stoicism, an ancient philosophy rooted in rationality and virtue, offers timeless wisdom for fathers seeking to navigate these conflicts with resilience and grace.

Infant Conflicts: Foundations of Patience

In the early years, conflicts with infants often revolve around basic needs and communication challenges. Stoicism encourages fathers to differentiate between what is within their control and what is not. When dealing with a crying infant, for example, recognizing that the infant's emotions are beyond direct control can help a father maintain composure. Stoicism teaches the virtue of patience, urging fathers to view these challenges as opportunities to cultivate inner strength and understanding.

Teen Conflicts: Nurturing Independence With Wisdom

As children transition into adolescence, conflicts can intensify as they grapple with identity, autonomy, and peer influences. Stoicism guides fathers to acknowledge the inevitability of these challenges and to approach them with a calm and rational mindset. Encouraging open communication becomes crucial, with Stoicism emphasizing the importance of understanding each child's unique perspective. Fathers can apply the Stoic principle of focusing on what is within their control—such as their own reactions and guidance—while allowing space for teens to navigate their developing sense of self.

Communication With Wisdom: A Message to Dads

For fathers seeking to enhance communication with their children, adopting a Stoic approach involves active listening and thoughtful responses. Stoicism underscores the value of empathy, prompting dads to understand their children's emotions and perspectives without imposing their judgments. By embodying the Stoic virtue of wisdom, fathers can provide guidance that aligns with both their values and the individual needs of their children.

Maintaining Calm: The Bedrock of Stoic Fatherhood

Stoicism places great emphasis on maintaining inner calm in the face of external challenges. Fathers can serve as Stoic role models by demonstrating emotional resilience. This not only sets a positive example for children but also creates a stable environment for navigating conflicts. By responding with calmness, fathers foster an atmosphere where open communication can thrive, allowing conflicts to be addressed constructively.

Stoic Strategies for Fatherhood Conflicts

- **Practice emotional detachment.** Stoicism encourages fathers to detach emotionally from external events and focus on their own responses. This allows for a more measured and thoughtful approach to conflicts, preventing impulsive reactions.

- **Cultivate mindfulness.** Mindfulness, a Stoic practice, involves being fully present in the moment. Fathers can apply this by actively listening to their children, understanding their needs, and responding with genuine attention.

- **Reflect and learn.** Stoicism encourages self-reflection. Fathers can continually assess their own reactions to conflicts, learn from experiences, and refine their approach to better align with Stoic principles. This ongoing process of reflection contributes to personal growth and improved father-child relationships.

Along the path of applying Stoic philosophy to family communication, we have explored how parents can cultivate patience, empathy, and wisdom to build stronger relationships with their children. However, it is essential to remember that as parents, we make inevitable mistakes. Perfection is an illusion and humility becomes an essential virtue on this journey.

Admitting our faults and sincerely apologizing to our children not only demonstrates humility, but also sets a valuable example. We teach our children that we are all constantly evolving beings, capable of learning and growing through our experiences. Every mistake is an opportunity for growth, and every challenge is a whetstone that shapes us. Open and honest communication, based on humility, strengthens family ties and fosters mutual understanding.

Achieving adequate communication dynamics in your family is a challenge that every dad will face at some point in his life. Family life involves becoming an expert in making agreements, being the champion of moderate expression, but at the same time learning when and how to prevail. It is not an easy task, but thanks to the valuable tools the Stoic approach gives you, achieving that goal becomes a little easier.

Looking ahead, the next chapter will explore the delicate balance between work and family responsibilities from a Stoic perspective. We will address how parents can apply Stoic principles to efficiently manage their work commitments without neglecting the family environment. We will explore strategies that allow parents to find harmony, maintain serenity, and be solid pillars for their families.

Chapter 7:

Work and Family—A Stoic Perspective

Work and family are two fundamental aspects of life that often present challenges and opportunities for people seeking balance and fulfillment. Stoic philosophy, rooted in ancient Greek philosophy and prominently advocated by thinkers such as Epictetus, Seneca, and Marcus Aurelius, offers valuable insights for navigating the complexities of work and family life.

Stoicism emphasizes the importance of cultivating virtue, wisdom, and inner strength to achieve a state of tranquility and well-being. Applying Stoic principles to work and family can provide a practical framework for managing responsibilities, relationships, and the inevitable ups and downs of life.

In the context of work and family, knowing your limitations means focusing efforts on actions and decisions that you can influence. For example, one can control one's work ethic, attitude, and responses to family dynamics, but external factors such as economic conditions or the behavior of others may be beyond one's control.

Stoicism teaches the importance of maintaining perspective, especially in the face of adversity. In the work context, setbacks or challenges may arise, and in family life, conflicts are inevitable. Stoicism advises people to see these challenges as opportunities for growth and learning. The central idea is to cultivate resilience and adapt to circumstances so that people can maintain a sense of inner calm and purpose.

Stoicism encourages living in harmony with nature, which, in the modern context, can be interpreted as aligning actions with the natural order of life. In the context of work and family, this means recognizing the cyclical nature of responsibilities and relationships. Work and family life have their seasons, and understanding the ebb and flow of these aspects can contribute to a more balanced and harmonious existence.

Stoicism encourages people to prioritize what really matters in life. In the context of work and family, this means recognizing the importance of both aspects and finding a balance that aligns with each person's values and priorities. It's about establishing clear priorities and boundaries, as the goal is to meet the demands of work and family without compromising your well-being.

A Stoic perspective on work and family underscores the importance of cultivating virtues, maintaining perspective, and aligning actions with the natural order of life. By practicing these principles, people can navigate the complexities of work and family with resilience, wisdom, and a sense of inner calm.

Stoic Principles Applied to Work and Family

As we have seen throughout the book, some of the concepts of Stoicism may not be applicable in modern-day life. However, in the difficult task of balancing your work with your family life, Stoic philosophy offers some interesting insights to think deeply about.

Stoicism provides timeless principles that can be applied to various aspects of life, including work and family. Next, I describe how Stoic principles can be applied to these important dimensions of human existence.

Stoicism teaches that the supreme good is virtue or moral excellence. Applied to work and family, this means that people must prioritize ethical conduct and integrity in both areas. In the workplace, practicing honesty, fairness, and diligence contributes to a virtuous work life. In the family, cultivating virtues such as compassion, patience, and understanding fosters healthy relationships.

The idea of accepting the present moment and embracing what is under our control is also present in these types of circumstances. In the context of work, this means focusing on the tasks at hand rather than worrying excessively about outcomes that are beyond our control. In family life, it means accepting the dynamics and challenges that arise from relationships and finding peace in the present moment.

This dichotomy of control encourages individuals to differentiate between what they can control and what they cannot. In the workplace, this means focusing on one's efforts, work ethic, and professional development, while recognizing that external factors, such as market fluctuations, are outside one's direct control. In family life, individuals can focus on their own attitudes and behaviors, recognizing that they cannot control the actions of others.

Stoicism teaches that challenges and adversity provide opportunities for personal and moral growth. In this way, in work and family life, conflicts and difficulties can serve as opportunities for people to develop patience, empathy, and stronger bonds with both loved ones and coworkers.

To do this, you need to remember the sense of moderation that encourages people to avoid excess and practice temperance. This means finding a balance between ambition and satisfaction, avoiding seeking success at the expense of well-being. This strategy allows you to maintain a healthy balance between personal activities and family commitments, without neglecting either or both.

Finally, a healthy balance between work and family life encourages dads to cultivate gratitude for present circumstances. Appreciate what you have instead of dwelling on what you lack. This applies both in work and in life. Gratitude becomes a necessary feeling to keep you from going crazy—by which I mean that, thanks to gratitude, you can truly value what you have.

And in the end, that's what Stoic parenting is all about.

The Challenge of Stoic Balance: The Nature Factor

The challenge of achieving Stoic balance at work and with family takes on a nuanced dimension when considering the influence of the nature factor. Rooted in the ancient philosophy of Stoicism, the pursuit of balance is enriched by aligning one's actions with the natural order of the world.

This involves recognizing the cyclical nature of both work and family, understanding the inherent ebb and flow of challenges and successes. Additionally, embracing the external environment and fostering harmony with nature becomes crucial, emphasizing sustainability and responsible resource use.

Stoicism encourages adaptability to change, viewing it as a natural aspect of life, whether in professional responsibilities or family dynamics. Mindful presence in nature serves as a source of inspiration and rejuvenation, fostering tranquility amid life's demands. Aligning daily routines with natural rhythms and acknowledging the seasons of life contribute to a balanced existence. Nature, viewed as a teacher of virtue, inspires the cultivation of endurance, adaptability, and interconnectedness in navigating the challenges of work and family.

To foster a harmonious balance between the demands of work and family life, people can effectively integrate nature-based principles into their daily routines through three key strategies.

1. First, it is essential to integrate the *healing power of nature* into everyday life. Consider incorporating short breaks outdoors, whether it's a quiet walk in a nearby park or a moment of serenity in a garden oasis. The sights, sounds, and scents of the natural world provide a therapeutic backdrop that allows for a mental reset and an opportunity to momentarily disconnect from the stresses of work and family responsibilities.

2. Second, embrace the concept of *adaptability* by drawing inspiration from the resilience observed in the natural world. Nature is inherently adaptable, weathering storms and evolving over several seasons. Similarly, people can face inevitable changes in professional and family life with a Stoic mindset. We talk about recognizing change as an inherent part of the natural order and, thus, cultivating a sense of acceptance and developing the mental strength to adapt to changing circumstances. This adaptability encourages a proactive approach to challenges, allowing people to respond with resilience and grace.

3. Finally, *express gratitude* as a transformative practice to foster a positive outlook on both the challenges and opportunities that work and family present. Inspired by the cyclical patterns observed in the natural world, people can recognize the value inherent in each stage of life. Expressing gratitude for challenges encountered contributes to personal growth and resilience, while recognizing opportunities fosters a sense of abundance and fulfillment.

Stoic Strategies to Integrate Into the Family Routine

Family Reflection Time

Instead of the traditional notion of individual reflection, consider introducing time dedicated to family reflection into your routine. Meet regularly with loved ones to openly discuss experiences, challenges, and joys.

This shared time of reflection aims to foster a collective understanding of each family member's perspectives, promoting empathy, unity, and a Stoic appreciation for the shared journey.

Foster an environment of open communication and active listening, creating a space where everyone feels heard and understood. This practice not only strengthens family ties but also aligns with Stoic values of mutual respect and shared wisdom.

Goals for Virtuous Families

Take family goal-setting beyond individual aspirations by encouraging virtuous family goal-setting. Set goals that align with Stoic virtues, such as wisdom, compassion, and resilience.

This collective approach fosters a shared sense of purpose and unity as the family works together to embody Stoic principles in daily life. Discuss and define specific actions that reflect these virtues, creating a roadmap for shared growth and development.

By properly concentrating your efforts on clear goals, the family reinforces its commitment to values that contribute positively to individual and collective well-being.

Eating Like a Stoic

Elevate the act of daily meals to a Stoic ritual by incorporating mindful practices. Encourage each family member to express gratitude for the nutrition provided and to share aspects of the day that align with Stoic principles. This intentional approach to eating promotes mindfulness and turns the experience of eating into an act of virtuosity.

It's about recognizing the importance of savoring the present moment, thereby fostering an atmosphere of appreciation and satisfaction. To transform mealtimes into a mindful experience, collectively embrace the Stoic principles of gratitude and living in the present.

Mindfulness for Children

Introduce age-appropriate Stoic mindfulness practices into the family routine, especially designed for children. Simple exercises like mindful breathing or expressing gratitude before bed can instill Stoic values from an early age.

Emphasize the importance of self-awareness and emotional resilience, providing tools that allow children to approach challenges with a mindful mindset. These practices in daily life contribute to the development, not only of individual mindfulness, but also of a collective atmosphere of calm and reflective interaction.

Stoic Acts of Kindness

Infuse Stoic principles into family dynamics by actively encouraging acts of kindness. Inspire family members to perform daily acts of generosity and compassion, aligning with the Stoic concept of positively contributing to the well-being of others.

Discuss and celebrate these acts together, fostering a sense of community and reinforcing the Stoic virtue of benevolence within the family. By consciously incorporating kindness into family interactions, each member contributes to creating a positive and supportive environment, reflecting Stoic values in action.

Stoic Work Values

Stoic philosophy, with its emphasis on virtue, resilience, and wisdom, offers a set of values that can significantly inform and enrich one's approach to work. Stoic work values invite individuals to cultivate a mindset that promotes professional excellence while maintaining a sense of inner tranquility. Here are key Stoic work values and their implications:

- **Virtue as the ultimate goal:** Stoicism places virtue as the highest good, and this principle directly applies to the workplace. Embracing virtue in work involves prioritizing moral excellence, integrity, and ethical conduct. Rather than being solely focused on external achievements, Stoic work values emphasize the importance of aligning professional actions with virtuous principles, contributing to a sense of purpose and fulfillment in one's career.

- **Endurance in the face of challenges:** Stoicism teaches the importance of enduring challenges with a calm and rational mindset. In the context of work, this involves approaching setbacks and difficulties with resilience and a commitment to continuous improvement. These values inspire individuals to see challenges not as obstacles, but as opportunities for personal and professional growth, contributing to a steady and composed desire in the workplace.

- **Acceptance of roles:** Stoicism emphasizes living in accordance with nature, which includes recognizing and accepting one's role in the professional sphere. Whether in a leadership position or a supportive role, embracing the responsibilities and duties of the job with mindfulness and acceptance contributes to a Stoic work ethic. This mindful approach fosters a sense of contentment and purpose, regardless of the specific role within the organization.

- **Integrity in professional relationships:** Stoic work values highlight the significance of cultivating virtuous relationships with colleagues, superiors, and subordinates. Integrity in professional interactions involves honesty, fairness, and a genuine concern for the well-being of others. By upholding ethical standards in the workplace, individuals contribute to a positive and harmonious work environment, reflecting Stoic principles of benevolence and social virtue.

- **Balancing ambition and contentment:** Stoicism encourages individuals to find a balance between ambitious goals and contentment with their current circumstances. While striving for professional excellence, Stoic work values emphasize the importance of appreciating the present moment and finding satisfaction in the pursuit of virtuous endeavors. This balance helps individuals avoid excessive attachment to external success, fostering a sense of inner tranquility.

Reflections on Quality of Life

Quality of life means to feel good in everyday life. Think of it as that pack that gives you good vibes both on a personal level and in your social role. And you know what? It's key to living a full and satisfying life. Now, this concept is not just about meeting basic needs, but about making your life as great as possible. And guess what? You are the boss of your own decisions!

Nowadays, when thinking about support, your needs, interests, and preferences are taken into account. It's like a personalized plan for you to achieve your goals and objectives. It's your time to shine! Now, the quality-of-life model that breaks it, according to Robert Schalock and Miguel Ángel Verdugo investigators from Hastings College and Universidad de Salamanca, has eight super-important dimensions. We talk about healthy relationships, personal development, emotional well-being, physical health, being the owner of your decisions, being financially calm, being part of the social movement, and having support (Linesa Ureña, 2021).

Stoic philosophy offers deep insights into the quality of life, emphasizing inner virtues, resilience, and a calm mindset. From a Stoic perspective, true well-being lies in focusing on virtue above external circumstances, cultivating qualities such as wisdom, courage, justice, and temperance. This approach involves accepting things that are out of our control, adapting to challenges with resilience, and practicing mindfulness to appreciate the present moment.

A Stoic life involves maintaining a detached view of external goods, recognizing their impermanence, and seeking inner satisfaction. Gratitude plays a crucial role in fostering awareness of the intrinsic value of life, encouraging people to appreciate their present circumstances. Stoicism also emphasizes the cultivation of social virtues and meaningful relationships, recognizing the interconnectedness of individuals within a community.

So now you know: Leading a quality life goes beyond having health and money in your wallet. It's about having control, feeling part of the movement, and having your rights respected. Stoicism encourages rational acceptance of external events and views adversity as an opportunity for personal growth. Develop resilience, so you'll not only overcome challenges effectively but also find a deeper sense of inner strength. Stoic philosophy teaches that happiness is not found in the pursuit of external achievements but in the practice of virtues and appreciation of what one already possesses.

A Personal Approach on Work-Life Balance

In every dad's life, where responsibilities pull at us from every direction and the demands of the world never cease, there exists a realm of unparalleled importance—the sanctum of family. For me, the path of a Stoic dad has been a resolute commitment to placing family above all else, an unwavering devotion that transcends the allure of professional triumphs and monetary gains.

Let me assure you, I've stood at the crossroads where enticing job opportunities beckoned with the promise of career zeniths, yet their shadows cast a looming threat upon the delicate balance of my domestic haven. It's in those pivotal moments that the Stoic philosophy breathed life into my decisions, reminding me that, in the grand scheme of existence, the sacred bonds of family are the bedrock upon which genuine happiness is built.

The clamor of societal expectations often sings the siren song of success, equating it with financial prowess and professional accolades. And yet, in the embrace of Stoicism, I found a counterpoint that resounds with clarity—the value of money diminishes when juxtaposed against the warmth and love of the family. It is not merely a matter of choosing between work and family; it is a conscious decision to wield one's professional pursuits as a tool to sculpt a life rich in familial connection and joy.

To some, this might seem an unconventional stance, a departure from the relentless pursuit of career ambitions that our economic system champions. But in the crucible of Stoic wisdom, I discovered a truth that resonates at the core of my being: The ephemeral nature of wealth and the transitory nature of professional roles pale in significance when compared to the enduring legacy of family love.

There were instances when I turned away from the glittering allure of job offers, fully cognizant that the price of financial gain might manifest in fractured family dynamics or distant relationships. It's a decision anchored in the Stoic principle of understanding what truly matters in life. For, what worth is prosperity if it only causes conflicts and uncertainties within the sanctuary of your own home?

As I share these reflections, it's not with the intent to prescribe a singular path, but, rather, to illuminate the understanding that the principles of Stoicism breathe life into our choices. The interpretation of these principles is a deeply personal voyage, shaped by the contours of individual circumstances and convictions. What I define as "living in the present" might echo differently in the hearts of other parents, each navigating their unique journey.

So, as you stand at the crossroads of career and family, contemplating the intricate dance between the demands of work and the joys of domesticity, let this be a gentle reminder: Money ebbs and flows, and jobs may change like seasons. But the sanctuary of family, with its laughter, shared moments, and unwavering support, stands as an irreplaceable constant.

Heed the wisdom of Stoicism—a guiding light that propels you to build not just a prosperous career, but a haven of love and connection within your family. Cherish your family, for in their embrace, you discover a wealth that transcends the temporal and echoes into eternity.

As seen in this chapter, quality of life, according to Stoic philosophy, is deeply intertwined with a virtuous life. This chapter evaluates the Stoic perspective on family relationships and their impact on overall happiness. Concluding with reflections on the search for meaning and satisfaction in both work and family, it encourages a holistic approach to life's activities. Stoicism guides us to recognize the intrinsic value of family ties and encourages contemplation of what really matters for a full existence.

The goal of this chapter is to delve deeper into the contemporary challenges surrounding this delicate balance and discover how Stoic philosophy can be a guiding light. Wisdom guides our choices, justice ensures a fair distribution of responsibilities, and temperance helps manage scarce resources of time and emotions.

The influence of modern work culture extends its reach into family life, often causing stress and burnout that strain family relationships. We saw the repercussions of these dynamics and emphasized the importance of finding a healthy balance.

Juggling work and family requires a conscious approach. Remember to explore the application of mindfulness in family moments and advocate for setting healthy boundaries. In addition, the importance of digital disconnection outside of working hours is emphasized. Learning to say "no" judiciously and adopting the art of delegation further contributes to a balanced and conscious lifestyle.

We must also recognize that raising children in a world full of career options and career challenges requires a Stoic touch. This chapter focuses on instilling Stoic values in parenting, teaching the importance of wisdom and courage in career decisions. It extends beyond individual growth, promoting justice and empathy in work environments. Real-life examples show how Stoic principles can be a positive force that enriches both work and family life.

As we delve deeper into the profound tapestry of Stoic fatherhood, the upcoming chapter unfurls the captivating theme of the legacy a Stoic father will leave behind. In this exploration, we embark upon a journey through the timeless principles and enduring virtues that, when embraced, not only shape the present but carve an indelible mark across the expanse of generations. In the pages ahead, we will uncover the artistry behind crafting a legacy rich in resilience, wisdom, justice, and love—a legacy that becomes a guiding light for those who follow.

Be prepared to be inspired and challenged to consider the enduring impact of your role as a Stoic father on the generations yet to come.

Chapter 8:

Stoic Fatherhood's Lifetime Legacy

Stoic parenting, when adopted as a guiding philosophy, has the power to create a lifelong legacy that transcends the boundaries of time and resonates through subsequent generations. It is not simply a set of principles applied in the moment, but a deliberate and conscious effort to instill lasting virtues that become the basis of the collective character of a family.

As a Stoic dad, you commit to the principles of wisdom, courage, justice, and temperance, and seek to strengthen the foundations of a legacy that will enrich and enliven family history. Every decision made in the crucible of daily life, from the mundane to the monumental, becomes a brushstroke of the masterpiece of a lifelong legacy.

At the heart of Stoic fatherhood is a Stoic father's legacy of equanimity in the face of challenges, thereby inspiring successive generations to face the storms of life with unwavering fortitude and an indomitable spirit. Furthermore, the Stoic father imparts the wisdom of distinguishing between what can be controlled and what cannot. This insight becomes a legacy of pragmatic optimism, teaching family members to focus their energy on shaping their responses to circumstances rather than futilely resisting the immutable forces of life.

In such a modern world, the legacy of a Stoic dad is a gentle reminder to savor the beauty of the now, fostering an environment where family members appreciate each other and the fleeting moments that make up a life well lived. Therefore, the Stoic dad's commitment to justice constitutes a cornerstone of the family legacya legacy of justice, empathy, and a moral compass that guides the family through ethical dilemmas. This commitment extends beyond mere words and finds expression in actions and demonstrations of love.

The legacy is a love not just spoken but lived, a testament to the Stoic understanding that love is not a fleeting emotion but a deliberate practice, an enduring force that unites family across time and space. Life must be transformed into a symphony of virtue, resilience, care, justice, and love. As the pages of the family's history unfold, the legacy of the Stoic father stands as a guiding light illuminating the path to a life of purpose, wisdom, and lasting connection. It is a gift passed down from generation to generation and an inheritance deeper than material wealth.

The Ultimate Stoic Dad

Ah, the "Ultimate Stoic Dad"! That kind of father who not only teaches you how to ride a bike, but also gives you a lesson in how to face life's unexpected turns with serenity. Parenting from the Stoic perspective is like raising a little philosopher in diapers—and, let me tell you, the results are amazing.

First of all, let's talk about the importance of being a Stoic parent. Imagine a man who does not allow himself to be swept away by the tumultuous waves of life, but floats calmly, showing his children that adversity is nothing more than an opportunity to demonstrate our inner strength. Being an "Ultimate Stoic Dad" involves cultivating virtue and self-discipline, teaching children that control over oneself is true freedom.

But why is this so essential? Because, dear reader, the influence of a Stoic father is like a gift that keeps on giving. Think about it: When we face challenges, aren't we guided by the values our parents instilled in us? Resistance in the face of adversity, acceptance of the uncontrollable, and the constant search for virtue are seeds that an "Ultimate Stoic Dad" sows in the hearts of his children.

Now, let me speak to you from experience, from that corner that few speak directly about: When you're a Stoic parent, it's not always about delivering philosophical sermons; sometimes it's just a matter of showing, not telling. Patience, the ability to stay calm in the midst of chaos, and focusing on what really matters are lessons that are conveyed more through actions than with words.

So, what are the essential characteristics of everything "Ultimate Stoic Dad"?

- **First, unwavering patience:** It's not just the patience of waiting for children to tie their shoes or put on their coat, but the patience of allowing them to make mistakes and learn from them, of being a beacon of calm in the midst of their emotional storms.

- **Second, compassionate empathy:** An "Ultimate Stoic Dad" not only understands that we are all human and make mistakes, but he also shows compassion toward those mistakes, guiding his children with love and without judgment.

- **And, finally, serene humility:** Recognizing that you don't always have all the answers and being willing to learn and grow alongside your children is a sign of true Stoic strength. It is not about having all the answers, but about being open to the constant search for wisdom and virtue.

So, to all the "Ultimate Stoic Dads" out there, continue to be that beacon of calm wisdom in the storm of life. Its lessons will resonate in the lives of your children long after they have flown the nest, reminding them that true strength is ultimately found in inner calm.

Your Traditions and Rituals

Creating traditions and rituals within your own family allows for a strong and lasting connection. These rituals are the heart of family life and ground everyone in a sense of belonging and continuity. Next are some reflections on the traditions and rituals that have taken root in my own family.

Family Movie Night

A much-loved tradition in our home is the weekly Family Movie Night. It's a time when everyone puts away their devices, gathers on the couch with comfy blankets, and enjoys a movie together. We take turns selecting the movie and create a rotating schedule that ensures everyone's tastes are taken into account. The joy is not just in the film itself, but in the shared laughter, arguments, and occasional debates over who gets to choose next.

Sunday Brunch

Sunday brunch has become a ritual that sets a positive tone for the week ahead. Whether we make a big breakfast together or head to our favorite lunch spot, this time allows us to reflect on the week behind us and discuss our plans for the week ahead. It is a relaxed, unhurried time that encourages open communication and a sense of unity.

Annual Family Retreat

Once a year, we embark on a family retreat. It could be a weekend getaway to the mountains, a beach vacation, or simply a staycation, and we explore our own city as tourists. This tradition serves as a reset button, offering us dedicated time to bond, reflect on the past year, and set intentions for the future. It's a powerful way to create lasting memories and strengthen our family bonds.

Gratitude Jar

In an age of constant activity, it's easy to overlook the small, beautiful moments in our daily lives. We keep a gratitude jar on the kitchen counter and each family member contributes notes expressing gratitude for something each week. On New Year's Eve, we gather to read these notes and reflect on the collective blessings and experiences that shaped our year. It is a simple ritual that cultivates mindfulness and appreciation.

Adventure Saturdays

To inject a sense of spontaneity and adventure into our lives, we have designated Saturdays as "Adventure Saturdays." This could mean exploring a nearby hiking trail, trying a new recipe together, or embarking on a day trip to a neighboring city. The goal is to break the routine and infuse a spirit of exploration into our weekends.

In cultivating these traditions and rituals, it's all about creating a family culture that reflects our values, strengthens our bonds, and provides a sense of continuity for both the present and the future. These rituals, big or small, become the stories we tell and the memories we treasure, shaping our family's identity.

Mastering the Art of Learning

Mastering the art of learning like a Stoic parent is akin to embarking on a lifelong journey of wisdom, resilience, and constant self-improvement. The Stoic approach to learning becomes a guiding philosophy, a compass that not only navigates the challenges of parenthood, but also shapes the character of the next generation. We were talking about this when we said that the need to be humble and trust in the learning process is key for every Stoic dad.

The Stoic dad understands that learning is an admission that there is always room for improvement. And you have that mentality. That's why you are here reading these words. He begins by acknowledging that no one has all the answers, and that each day provides opportunities to refine one's understanding of oneself and the world. Ask yourself what activity you have more than 10,000 hours of experience in to consider yourself an expert, and in everything else practice moderation and humility. This attitude becomes the foundation for modeling a growth mindset for children, fostering an environment where curiosity and the pursuit of knowledge is celebrated.

Taking pauses allows for reflection. Allow yourself to analyze and draw valuable lessons from daily experiences—you owe it to yourself as a man and as a father. As you interact with children, recognizing that each interaction is an opportunity to learn more about their evolving personalities and needs, you also open enough space in your mind and heart to learn from them.

Children learn more from what they see than from what they are told, and a Stoic dad understands the importance of leading by example. Whether demonstrating a commitment to continuous learning or modeling emotional intelligence during difficult times, actions speak louder than words. The Stoic dad becomes a living testimony of the principles of virtue and self-improvement.

While Stoicism provides a solid foundation for dealing with life's complexities, a Stoic parent also recognizes the importance of flexibility. Parenting requires adaptability, and the ability to adjust one's approach while remaining true to Stoic principles is a delicate balance. This flexibility allows for a more nuanced understanding of each child's unique needs and characteristics.

The Stoic dad uses virtue as a compass when making decisions. When faced with options, the question goes from "What is convenient?" to "What is virtuous?" This prioritization of virtue becomes a cornerstone for teaching children the importance of ethical decision-making and the lasting value of aligning actions with one's core principles.

By mastering the art of learning like a Stoic parent, the trip becomes a shared experience with the family. The Stoic principles of humility, mindfulness, resilience, leading by example, balance, and prioritizing virtue create a framework for a rich and purposeful family life. Through this journey, the Stoic dad not only becomes a lifelong learner but also a wise guide, nurturing the seeds of virtue in the hearts of his children. The art of learning, seen through the lens of Stoicism, becomes a legacy, a gift that transcends generations.

Meditations: From Marcus Aurelius to You

Meditations offers a fascinating bridge between the past and the present, and every Stoic dad lives by connecting the timeless wisdom of Marcus Aurelius with the complexities of modern life. The personal writings of this ancient Roman emperor, captured in the memoirs he never thought someone else would read, resonate with surprising relevance, proposing the idea that the principles of a virtuous life are not ephemeral, but eternal.

Immersing ourselves in the pages of the *Meditations* allows us to find deep reflections on human nature, self-control and the purpose of life. These thoughts, originating in Marcus Aurelius' crucible of experiences, reveal an intrinsic connection to the challenges and aspirations of modern life. The pursuit of virtue, facing adversity, and the importance of authenticity are themes that transcend the ages, particularly resonating in the hearts and minds of those seeking a meaningful life.

The contemporary relevance of the *Meditations* highlights the perennial human need for guidance and wisdom. Marcus Aurelius, though separated from us by centuries, becomes a virtual advisor, a philosophical friend who offers perspectives on life, death, and the pursuit of virtue. His thoughts transcend temporal and geographical barriers, demonstrating the unique ability of ancient wisdom to resonate with universal human experience.

Thinkers of the past, such as Marcus Aurelius, not only provide us with a glimpse into the complexities of their lives, but also act as beacons illuminating our path. In a modern world often overwhelmed by the speed of change and the avalanche of information, the wisdom of the ancients acts as a reminder of the timelessness of fundamental truth.

The influence of these figures from the past lies not only in their historical achievements, but in the ability of their thoughts to trigger personal transformation. As we reflect on Marcus Aurelius' *Meditations*, we realize that these writings are not only accounts of his life, but also invitations to self-reflection and continuous improvement. They are a testament that the pursuit of virtue knows no temporal or cultural limits, and that the wisdom of the past can be a valuable ally on our personal journey.

The idea of this section is to remember that ancient wisdom is not simply a reliquary of the past, but a bridge to a more meaningful life in the present. It invites us to draw on the wealth of experience accumulated over the centuries and challenges us to apply the timeless lessons of Marcus Aurelius in our own pursuit of a virtuous life. In this dialogue between eras, we find not only a link with the past, but also a valuable guide for the present and the future.

Conclusion

As the curtain falls on this exploration of Stoic principles in the realm of family life, allow me to guide you toward the conclusion of this meaningful journey. In the tapestry of family existence, where each thread weaves a narrative of shared experiences and enduring connections, Stoicism stands as the fabric that not only sustains, but embellishes the fabric itself.

The cultivation of virtues, the center of Stoicism, makes us architects of a legacy built on indelible pillars. This legacy, palpable in the character of our children and future generations, transcends time, leaving an imprint that lasts over the years.

In a world where uncertainty looms, Stoicism gives our children the strength to face life's storms with grace and fortitude. The legacy we leave is a reminder that challenges are not insurmountable obstacles, but rather opportunities to grow and discover yourself. Our children inherit a mindset that values every fleeting moment, creating a family culture in which the present is celebrated and embraced.

Additionally, Stoicism teaches the art of discernment, guiding our children to distinguish between what they can and cannot control. This wisdom becomes your compass in the midst of uncertainties, fostering a legacy of pragmatic optimism.

The benefits extend to justice: a commitment to fairness and moral integrity. We forge a legacy in which ethical considerations guide our decisions, passing on to our children a firm moral compass in the face of life's ethical dilemmas.

Ultimately, the virtuous life espoused by Stoicism leaves a legacy of love—a love that is not only professed but lived; a love that transcends the boundaries of life itself. In the sanctuary of a Stoic family, love becomes a force that unites generations, a lasting legacy that resonates through the centuries.

As we reflect on the benefits of Stoicism in family life, let us recognize the profound impact our choices and values have on the legacy we leave our children. Stoicism is not just a philosophical stance; it is a gift of wisdom, resilience, mindfulness, justice, and love, a legacy that is a testimony to a life well lived and a family deeply loved.

It is crucial to emphasize that incorporating Stoic philosophy into our daily lives is not a quick fix, but rather a long-lasting process that requires patience, perseverance, and a strong will over time.

Stoicism, as embodied in the reflections of Marcus Aurelius, is not a magical elixir that promises instant transformation. It is a philosophical framework that invites us to cultivate virtues, embrace resilience, and navigate the complexities of life with a calm mind. This process requires a commitment that transcends the attractiveness of immediate results.

It is essential to recognize that the journey toward a Stoic lifestyle is a marathon, not a sprint. The timeless wisdom of Stoicism is a guide, not a shortcut. It requires a daily practice of self-awareness, conscious decision-making, and a continuous effort to align our actions with virtuous principles.

Furthermore, incorporating Stoic philosophy into daily life is an exercise in temperance: the moderation of desires, patience in the face of challenges, and the deliberate cultivation of resilience. It's about recognizing that setbacks and trials are inevitable, but that our response to them is within our control.

Let us remember that courage is the cornerstone of a Stoic life. It takes courage to confront our shortcomings, confront the uncertainties of the future, and persist in the pursuit of a virtuous existence. This courage is not a one-time decision, but a constant choice we make, day after day, in the face of triumphs and tribulations.

Your journey is unique, and every step you take toward virtue contributes to the masterpiece of a life well lived. May your efforts be the catalyst for lasting change and may Stoic wisdom be a loyal companion on your path.

Now, I invite you, dear reader, to put these principles into practice. Apply them to your daily life, guide your children with Stoic wisdom, and let the legacy you build be a source of inspiration to those around you. Remember that transforming your life and your parenting style can be challenging, but consistency, focus, and a positive attitude are the keys that open the doors to lasting transformation.

On this journey, be a conscious architect of your legacy, building not only for the present, but for generations to come. May your path be illuminated by the serene light of Stoicism, guiding you toward a life of meaning, connection, and enduring love. Go forth and carve your Stoic legacy into your family's history!

References

¿Qué son las virtudes estoicas y aristotélicas? (n.d.). Quora. Retrieved December 30, 2023, from https://es.quora.com/Qu%C3%A9-son-las-virtudes-estoicas-y-aristot%C3%A9licas

A Mindfulness Practice for Stressed-Out Parents. (2019, June 13). Mindful. https://www.mindful.org/when-parenting-gets-tough/

A Stoic Approach to Parenting: Helping Parents and Kids Thrive by Meredith Alexander Kunz. (2021, January 2). Modern Stoicism. https://modernstoicism.com/a-stoic-approach-to-parenting-helping-parents-and-kids-thrive-by-meredith-alexander-kunz/#:~:text=Stoic%20parenting%20philosophy%20focuses%20on

Británica, E. (2020). *Zeno of Citium | Hellenistic philosopher* | Britannica. In Encyclopædia Britannica. https://www.britannica.com/biography/Zeno-of-Citium

Daily Stoic. (2019, February 6). *What Is Stoicism? A Definition & 9 Stoic Exercises To Get You Started.* Daily Stoic. https://dailystoic.com/what-is-stoicism-a-definition-3-stoic-exercises-to-get-you-started

Dichter, R. (2017). *Epictetus Online: Taking a Stoic Approach to Social Media.* Gadfly. https://www.thegadflymagazine.org/home-1/2017/4/10/epictetus-online-taking-a-stoic-approach-to-social-media

Dzotsi, E. (2023, June 29). *Balance and Stoicism: Seeking Equilibrium or Indifference?* Medium. https://erycked.medium.com/balance-and-stoicism-seeking-equilibrium-or-indifference-9cd7f0e7e61

Estoicismo para Niños. (n.d.). Ninos.kiddle.co. Retrieved December 30, 2023, from https://ninos.kiddle.co/Estoicismo

Estoicos.club, R. (2023, May 19). *Cómo enseñar a tus hijos sobre el estoicismo.* https://estoicos.club/como-ensenar-a-tus-hijos-sobre-el-estoicismo/

14 Ways To Create Your Stoic Daily Routine. (n.d.). Www.stoic-Buddy.com. Retrieved December 30, 2023, from https://www.stoic-buddy.com/blog/create-a-daily-stoic-routine

Hardy, M. (n.d.). *Importance of Family Communication.* LoveToKnow. https://www.lovetoknow.com/life/relationships/importance-family-communication

Harris, D. S. (2021, June 20). *It Is Well To Be Flexible.* Socrates Café. https://medium.com/socrates-cafe/it-is-well-to-be-flexible-f7ee6372b28a

Heng, S. (2023, May 9). *Modern Parenting: Challenges and Rewards.* OrbRom Center. https://orbrom.com/modern-parenting/#:~:text=One%20of%20the%20biggest%20challenges

How Family Traditions Can Help Build Stronger Bonds. (n.d.). Verywell Family. https://www.verywellfamily.com/family-rituals-meaning-examples-3288187

How To Teach Your Children About Stoicism. (2020, January 9). Daily Stoic. https://dailystoic.com/teach-children-stoicism/

Justice: The Most Important Virtue. (2020, March 2). Daily Stoic. https://dailystoic.com/justice-the-most-important-virtue/

MacRae, B. (2023, May 21). *Stoic Parenting: 6 Life Lessons From A New Father.* The Mindful Stoic. https://mindfulstoic.net/stoic-parenting-6-life-lessons-from-a-new-father/

Madrid, F. A. (2021, February 26). *¿A qué nos referimos cuando hablamos de "calidad de vida"?* Autismo Madrid. https://autismomadrid.es/noticias/a-que-nos-referimos-cuando-hablamos-de-calidad-de-vida/

Meditation For Kids. (n.d.). Headspace. Retrieved December 30, 2023, from https://www.headspace.com/es/meditation/kids

Meditations by Marcus Aurelius: Book Summary, Key Lessons and Best Quotes. (2018, March 31). Daily Stoic. https://dailystoic.com/meditations-marcus-aurelius

Salzgeber, J. (2017, December 15). *10 Practical Stoic Exercises for a Modern Stoic Lifestyle.* NJlifehacks. https://www.njlifehacks.com/10-practical-stoic-exercises-for-modern-stoic-lifestyle/

Sherman, N. (2021). *Stoic Wisdom: Ancient Lessons for Modern Resilience.* In *Amazon* (1st edition). Oxford University Press. https://www.amazon.com/Stoic-Wisdom-Ancient-Lessons-Resilience/dp/0197501834

Staff, M. (2020, June 11). *Mindfulness for Kids.* Mindful. https://www.mindful.org/mindfulness-for-kids/#:~:text=A%20Definition%20of%20Mindfulness%20Meditation

Standridge, P. (2018, November 17). *Virtue of temperance can offer life balance | DOLR.org.* Catholic Diocese of Little Rock. https://www.dolr.org/article/virtue-temperance-can-offer-life-balance

Stoics, M. M. (2023, July 19). *The Origins of Stoicism: A Deep Dive into Ancient Philosophy.* Modern Mind Stoics. https://modernmindstoics.com/2023/07/19/the-origins-of-stoicism-a-deep-dive-into-ancient-philosophy/

Stream, C. (2022, November 27). *Stoicism, Parenting, Flourishing.* Stoicism — Philosophy as a Way of Life. https://medium.com/stoicism-philosophy-as-a-way-of-life/stoicism-parenting-flourishing-49460e6a6b0a

Sutton, J. (2020, October 7). *Understanding Emotions: 15 Ways To Discover What You're Feeling.* PositivePsychology.com. https://positivepsychology.com/understanding-emotions/

The Autobiography of Benjamin Franklin. (1995). Www.ushistory.org. https://www.ushistory.org/franklin/autobiography/page04.htm

The Great Courses. (n.d.). www.thegreatcourses.com. Retrieved December 30, 2023, from https://www.thegreatcourses.com/courses/think-like-a-stoic-ancient-wisdom-for-today-s-world

The stoic parent: 10 Commandments for becoming a better parent. (n.d.). Daily Stoic Store. Retrieved December 30, 2023, from https://store.dailystoic.com/products/the-stoic-parent-10-commandments-for-becoming-a-better-parent-2

3 Stoic strategies for becoming happier. (n.d.). ThoughtCo. Retrieved December 30, 2023, from https://www.thoughtco.com/stoic-strategies-for-becoming-happier-3988010

What is conscious Parenting? (n.d.). Cleveland Clinic. Retrieved December 30, 2023, from https://health.clevelandclinic.org/conscious-parenting

What is stoicism philosophy? (n.d.). Www.myenglishpages.com. https://www.myenglishpages.com/english/reading-stoicism.php

Wisdom for fathers. (n.d.). Wisdom Hunters. Retrieved December 30, 2023, from https://www.wisdomhunters.com/product/wisdom-for-fathers/

Zamorano, E. (2022, July 8). *Lecciones estoicas para enseñar a tus hijos a superar las dificultades y no tener miedo a nada.* Elconfidencial.com. https://www.elconfidencial.com/alma-corazon-vida/2022-07-08/estoicismo-lecciones-ninos-educacion-hijos_3449342/

Printed in Dunstable, United Kingdom

77025437R00077